50 Fabulous Flowers
Volume 4

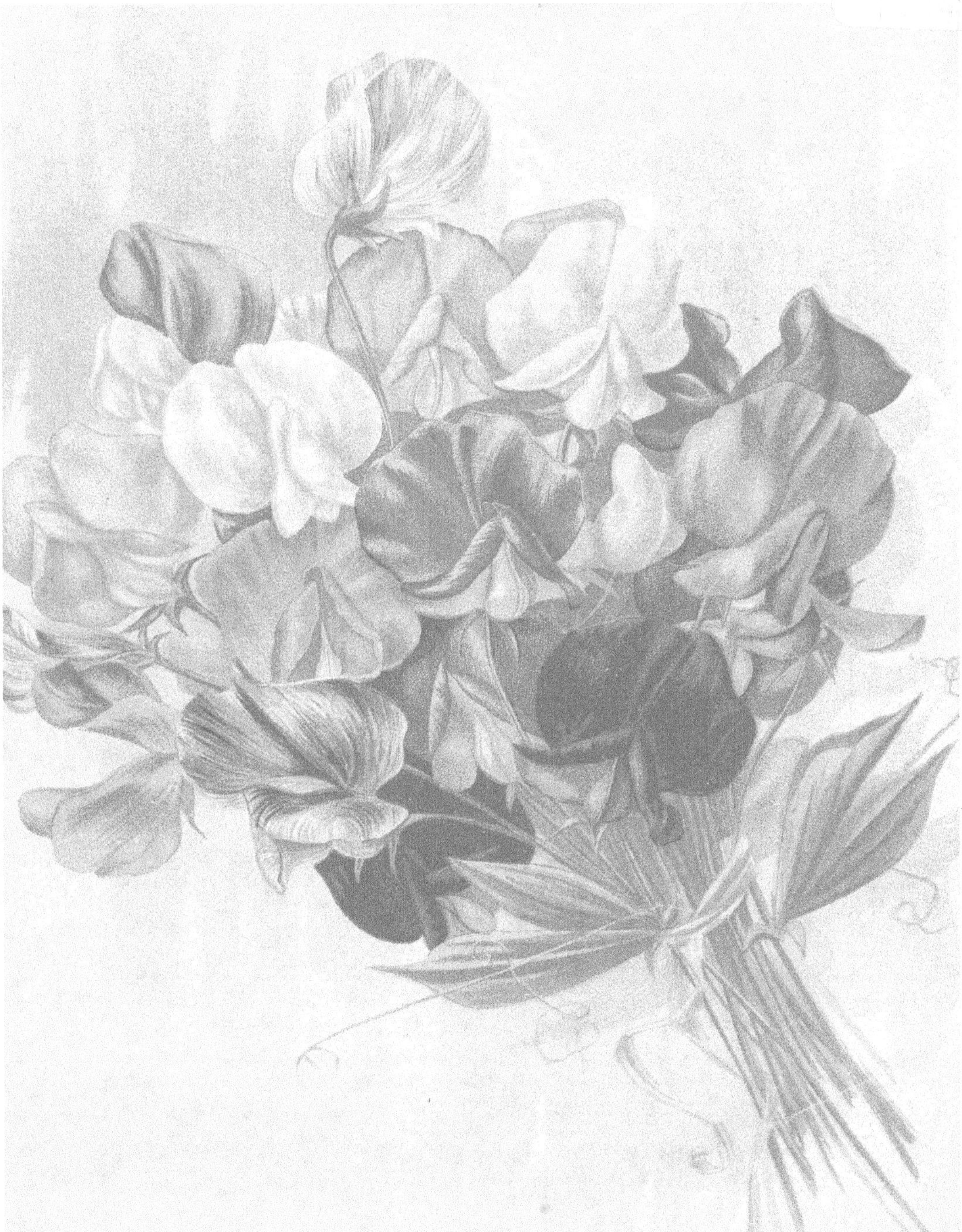

Hours of Creative Fun
Garden Press

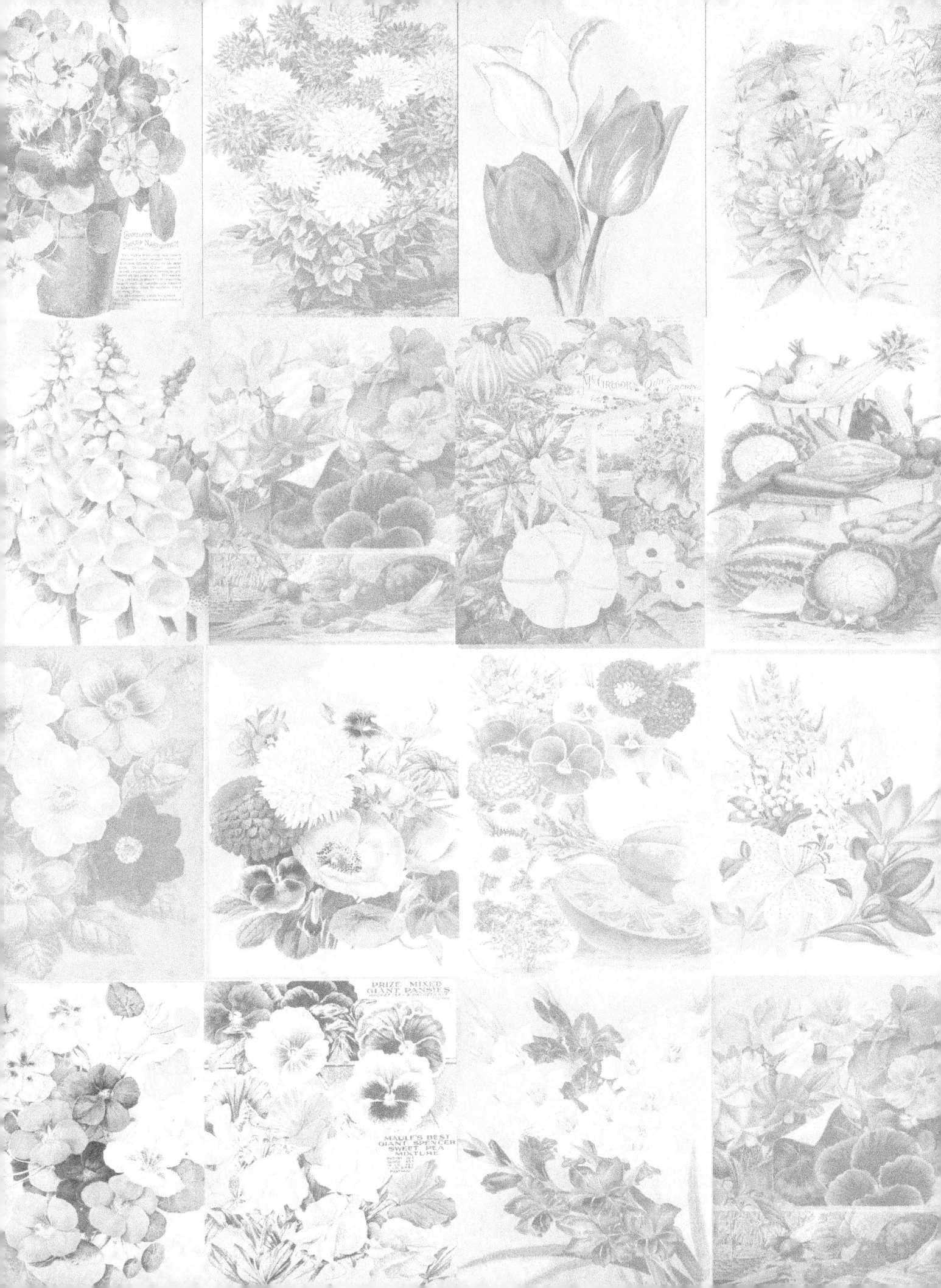

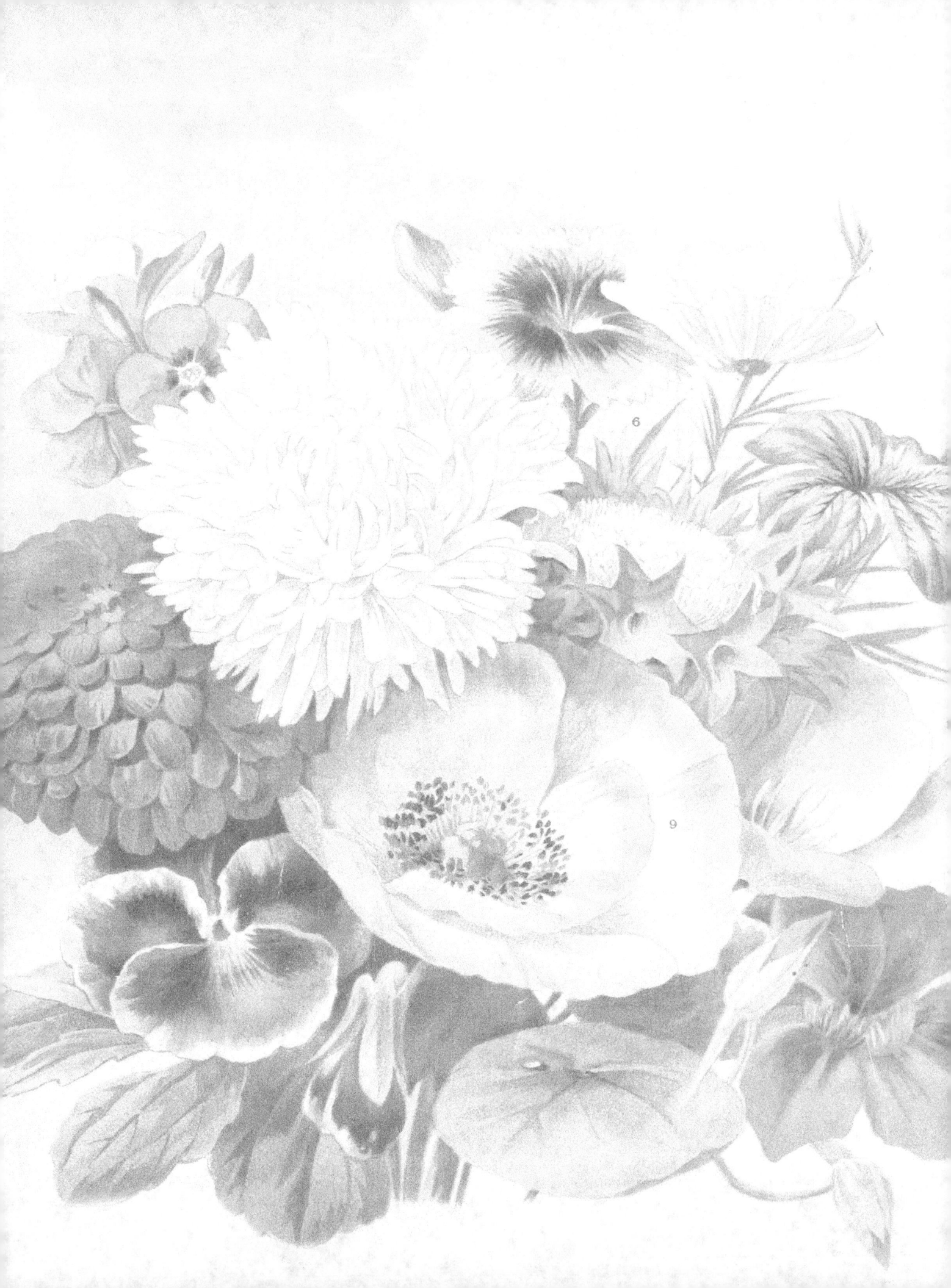

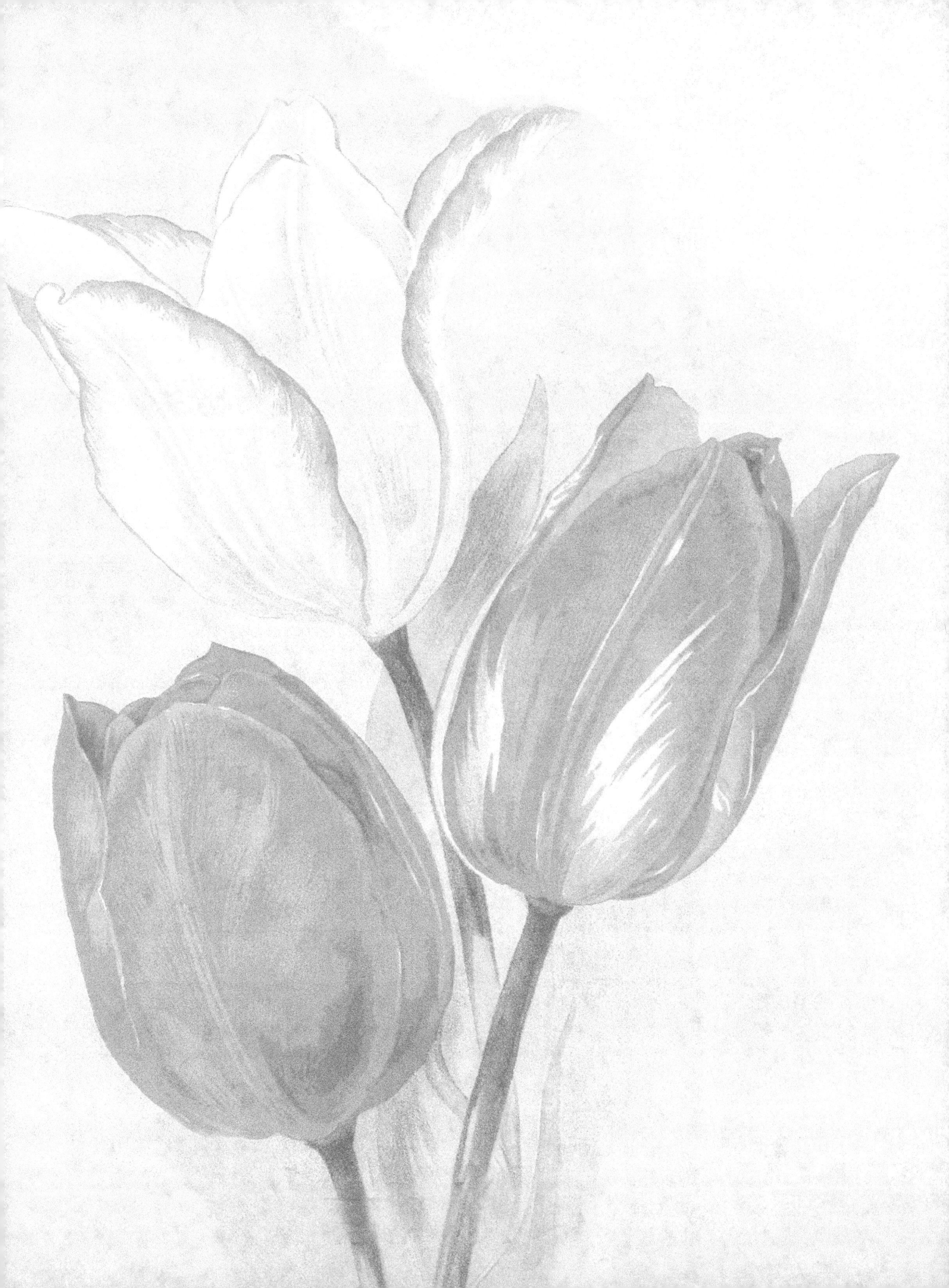

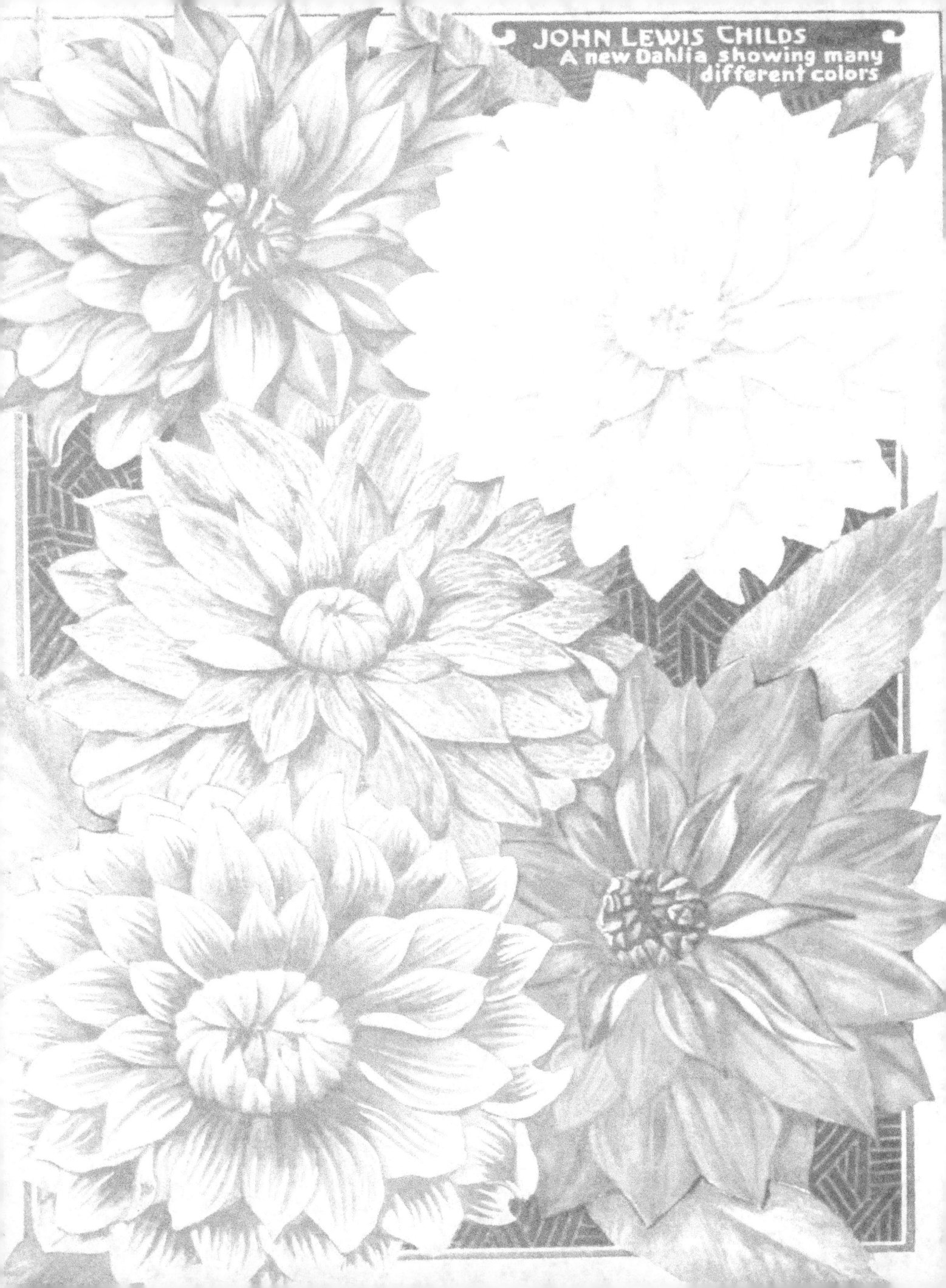

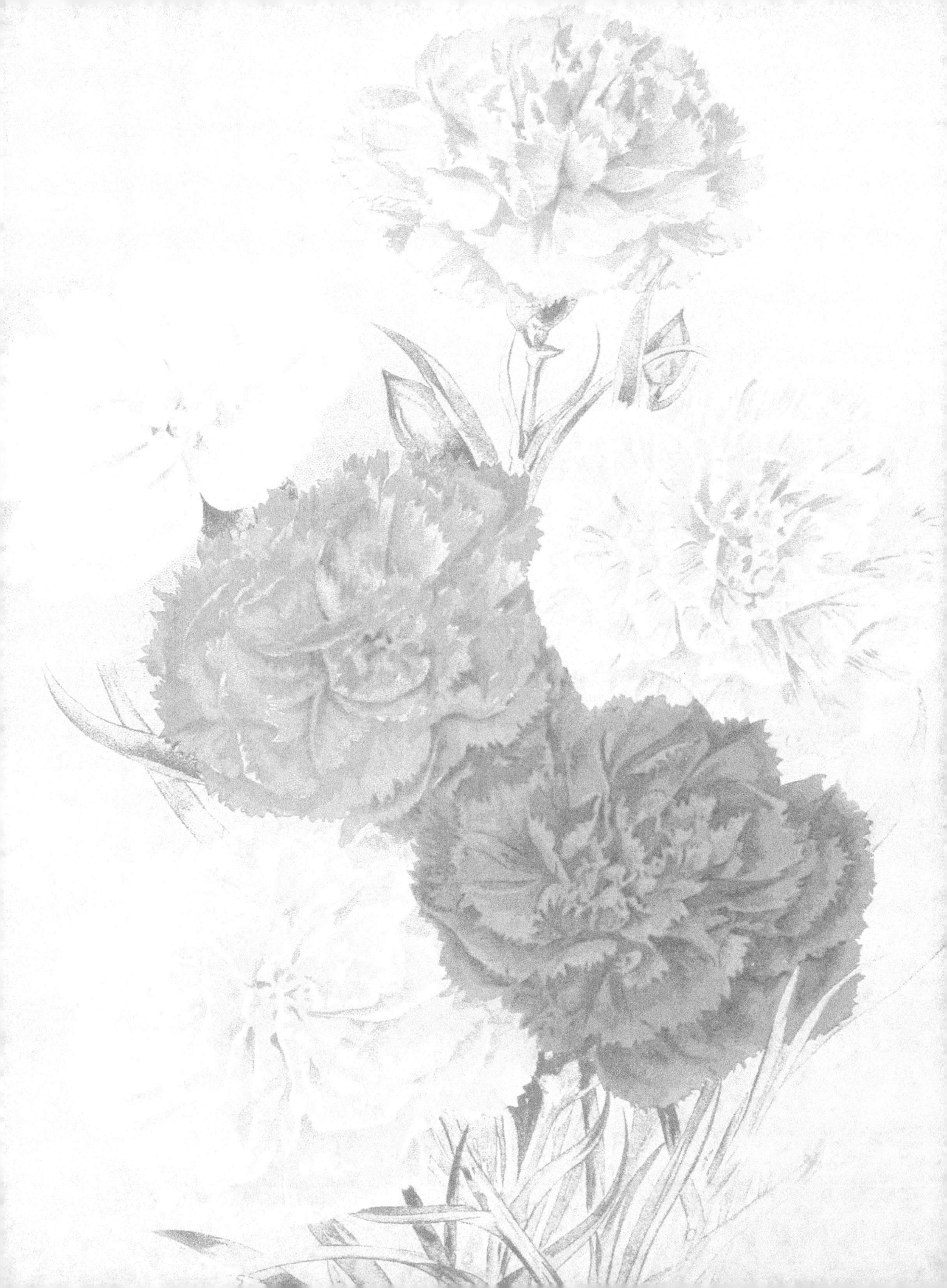

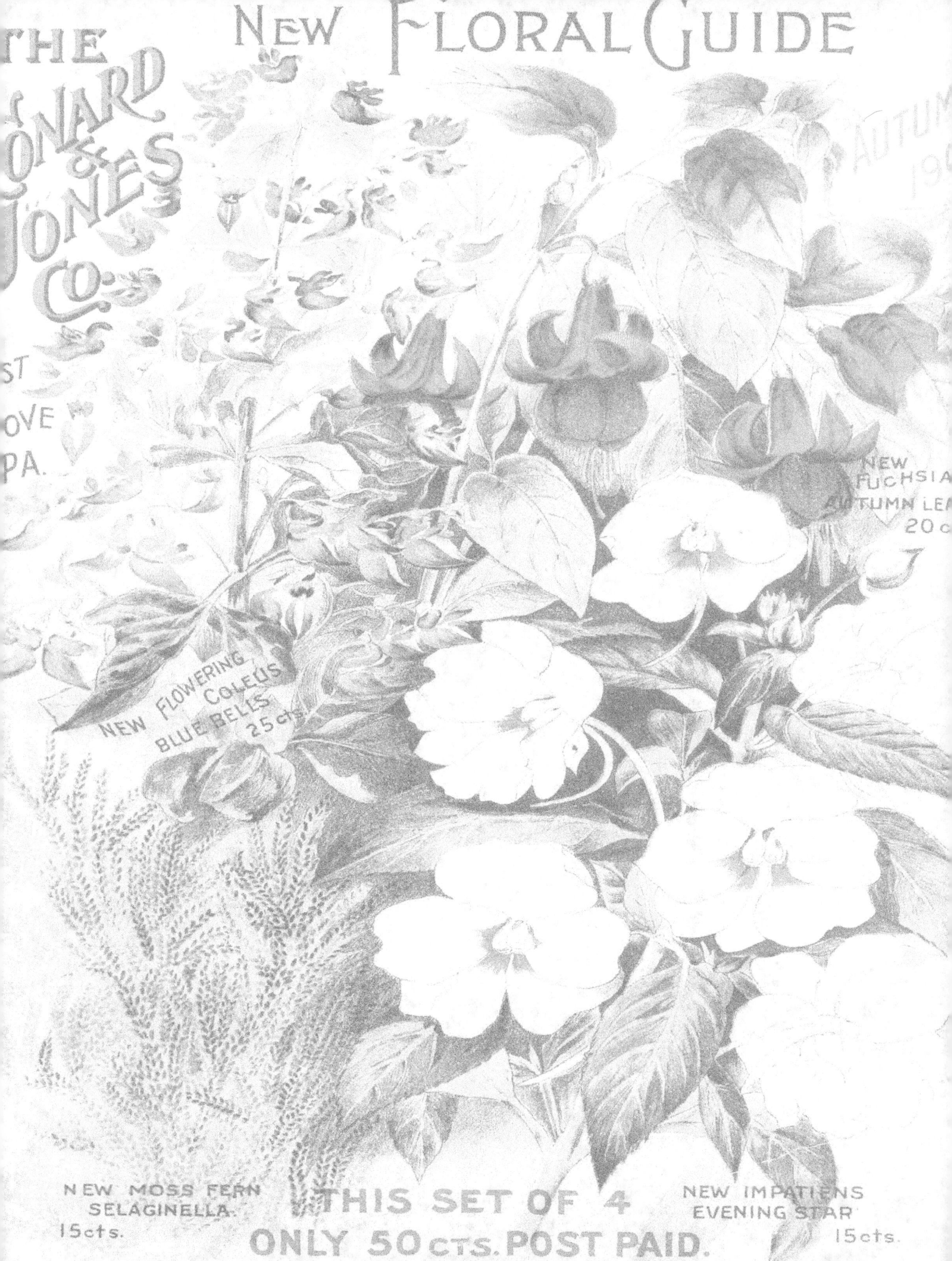

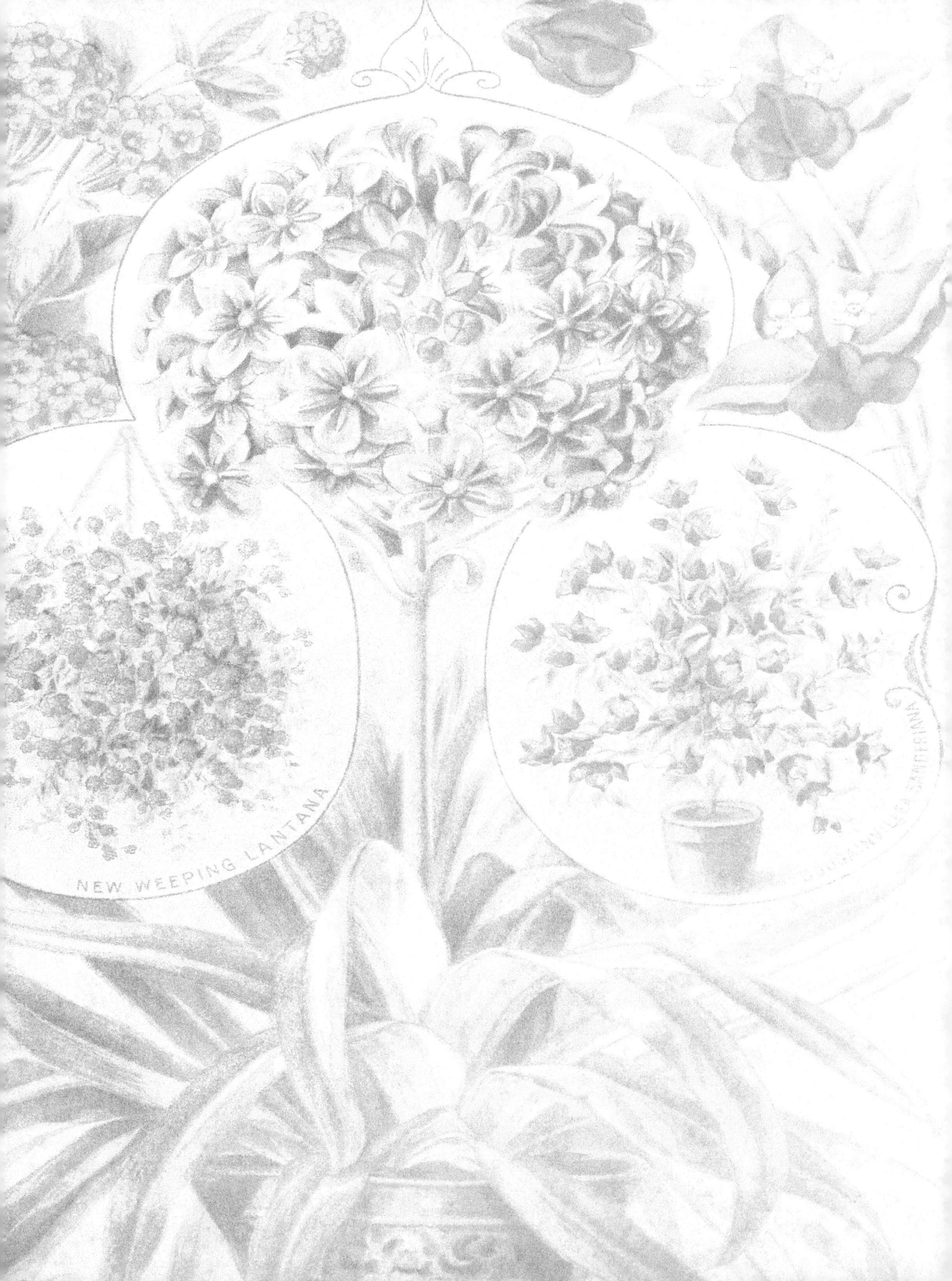

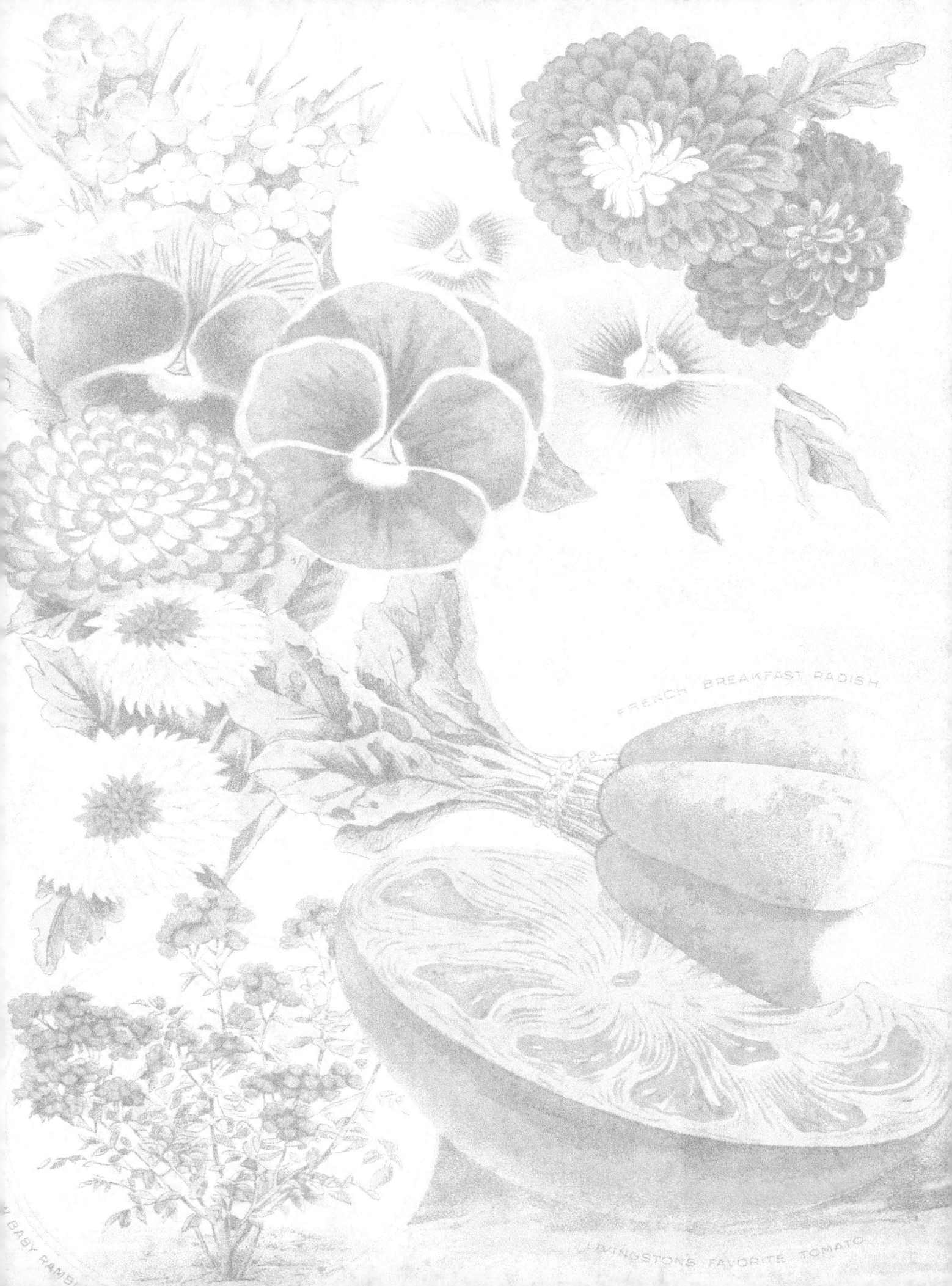

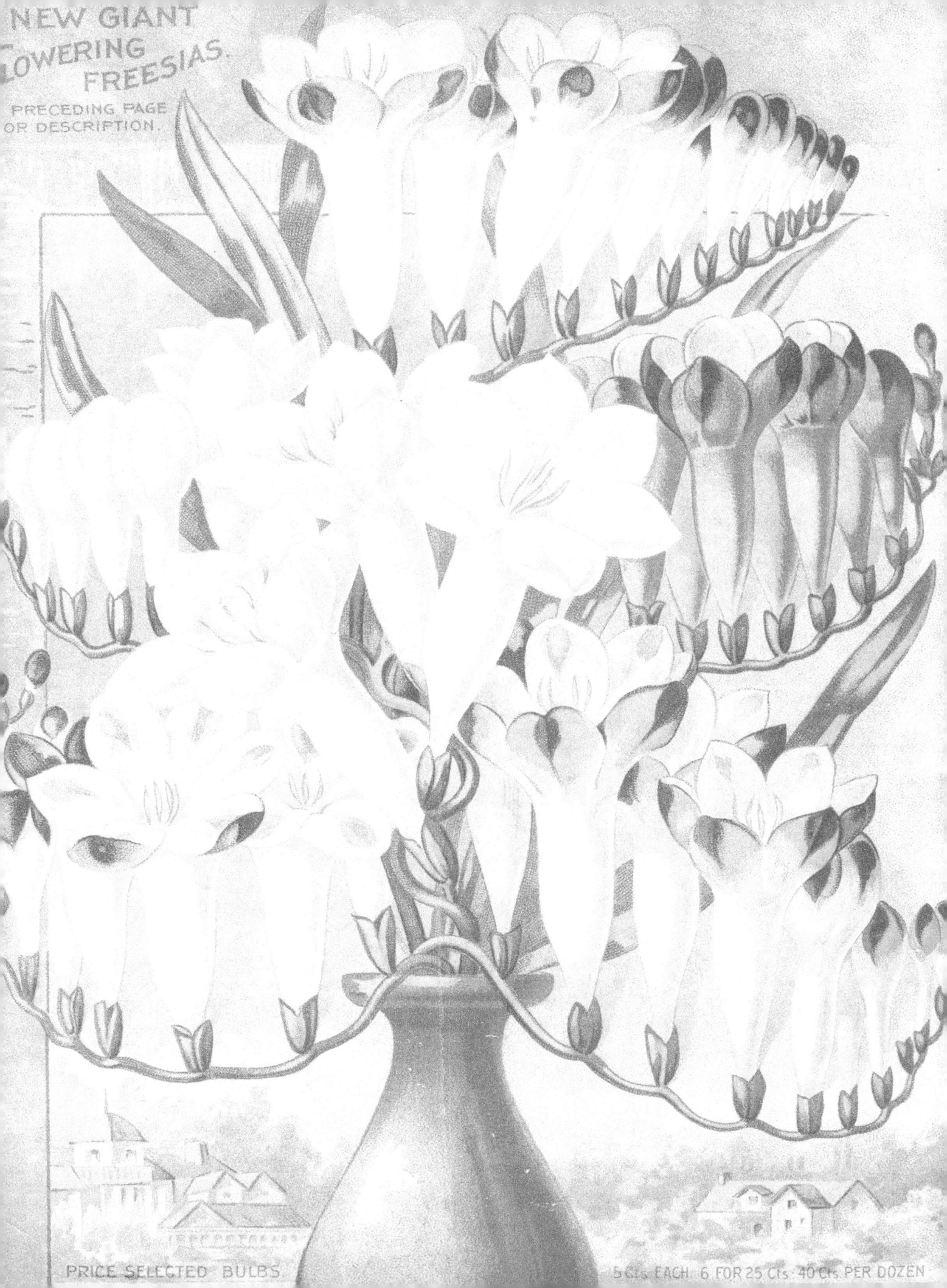

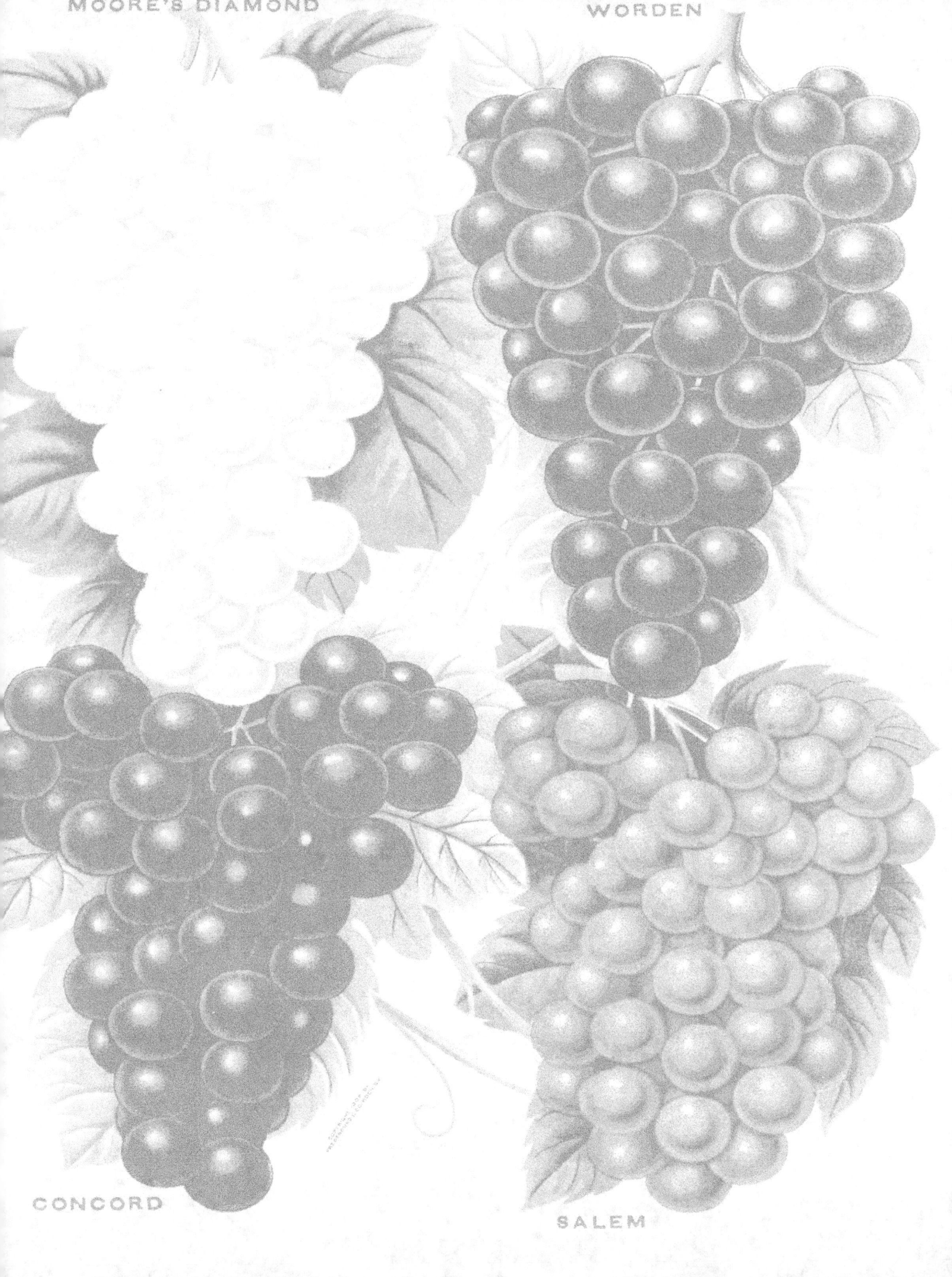

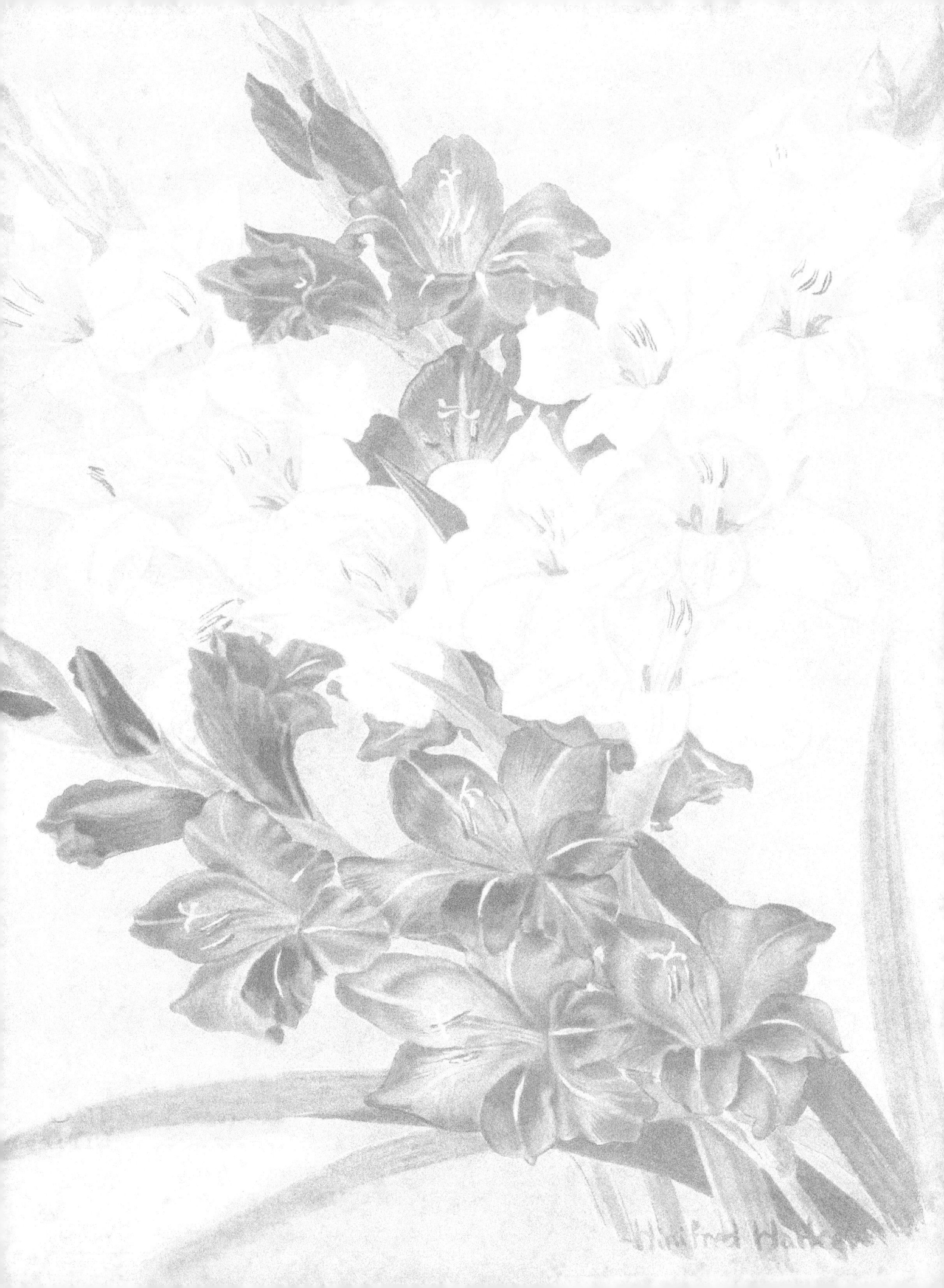

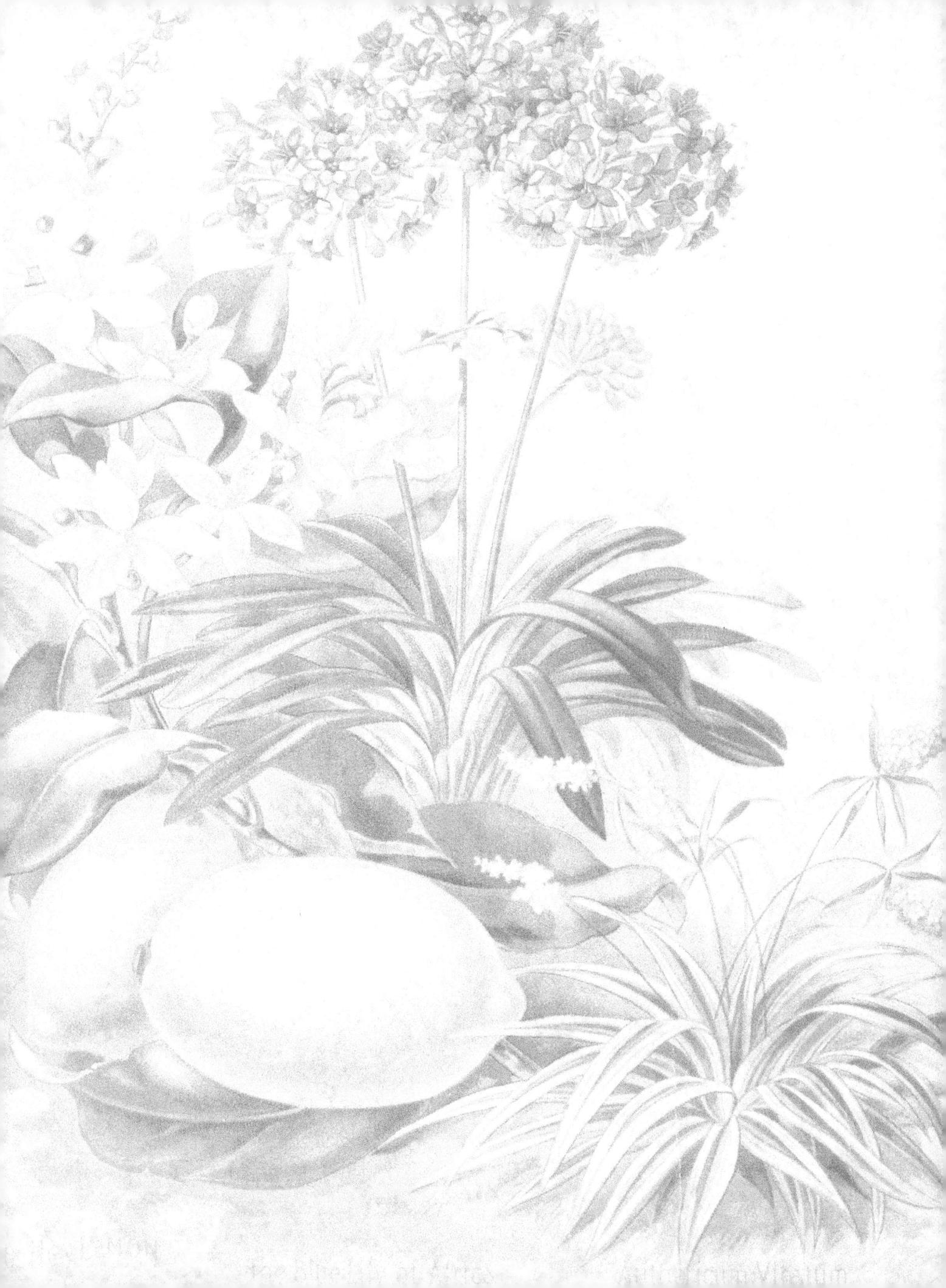

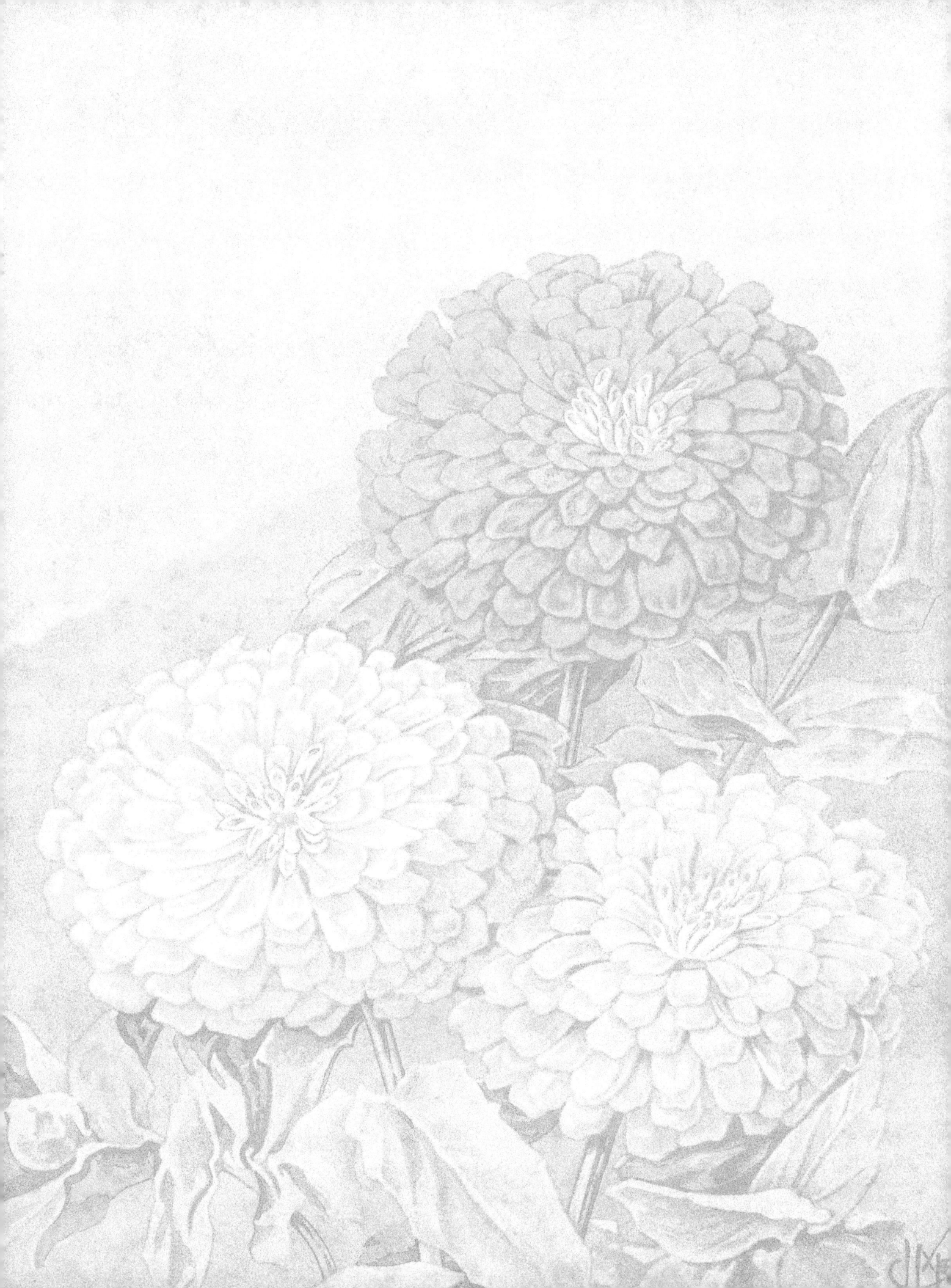

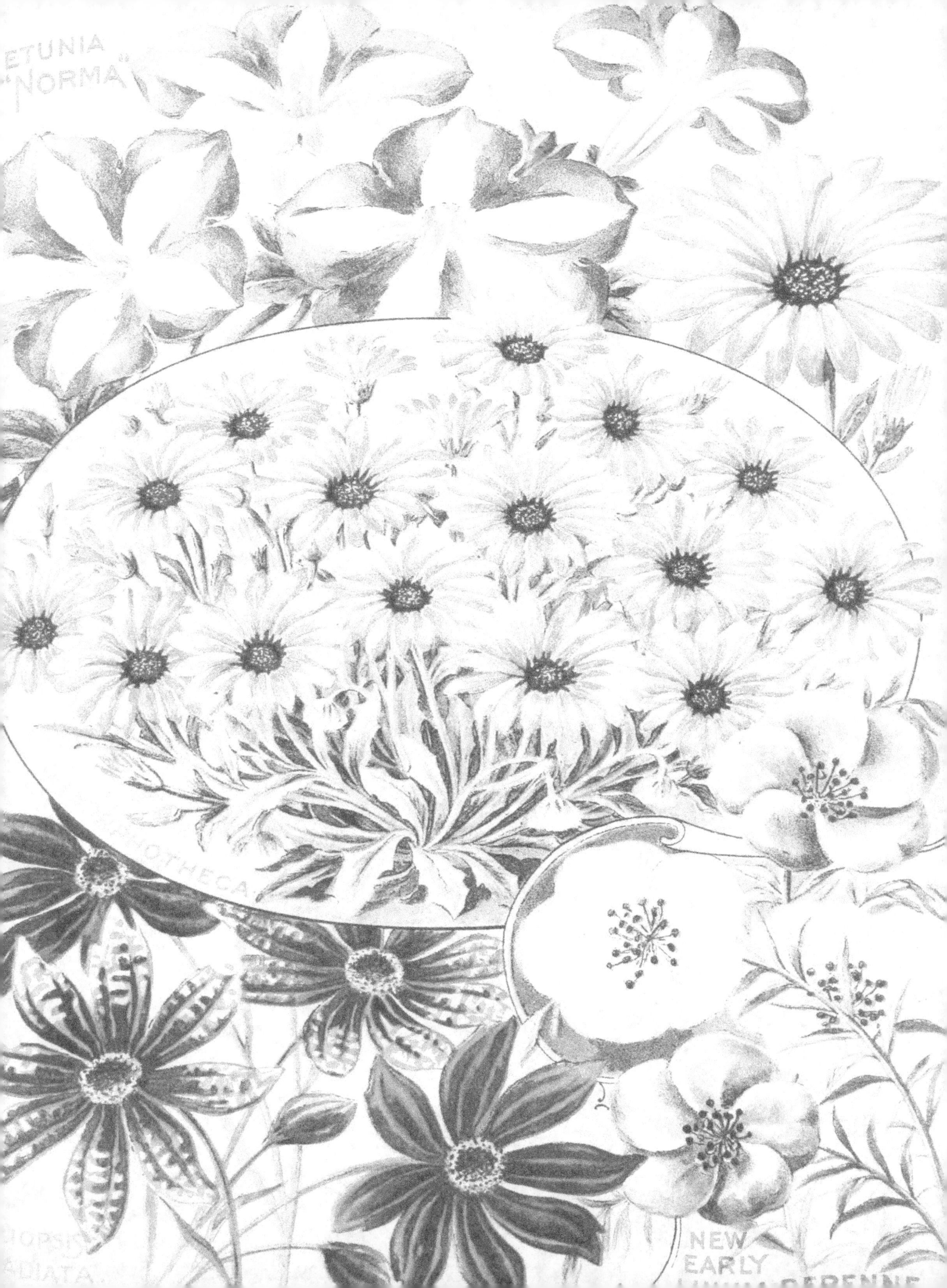

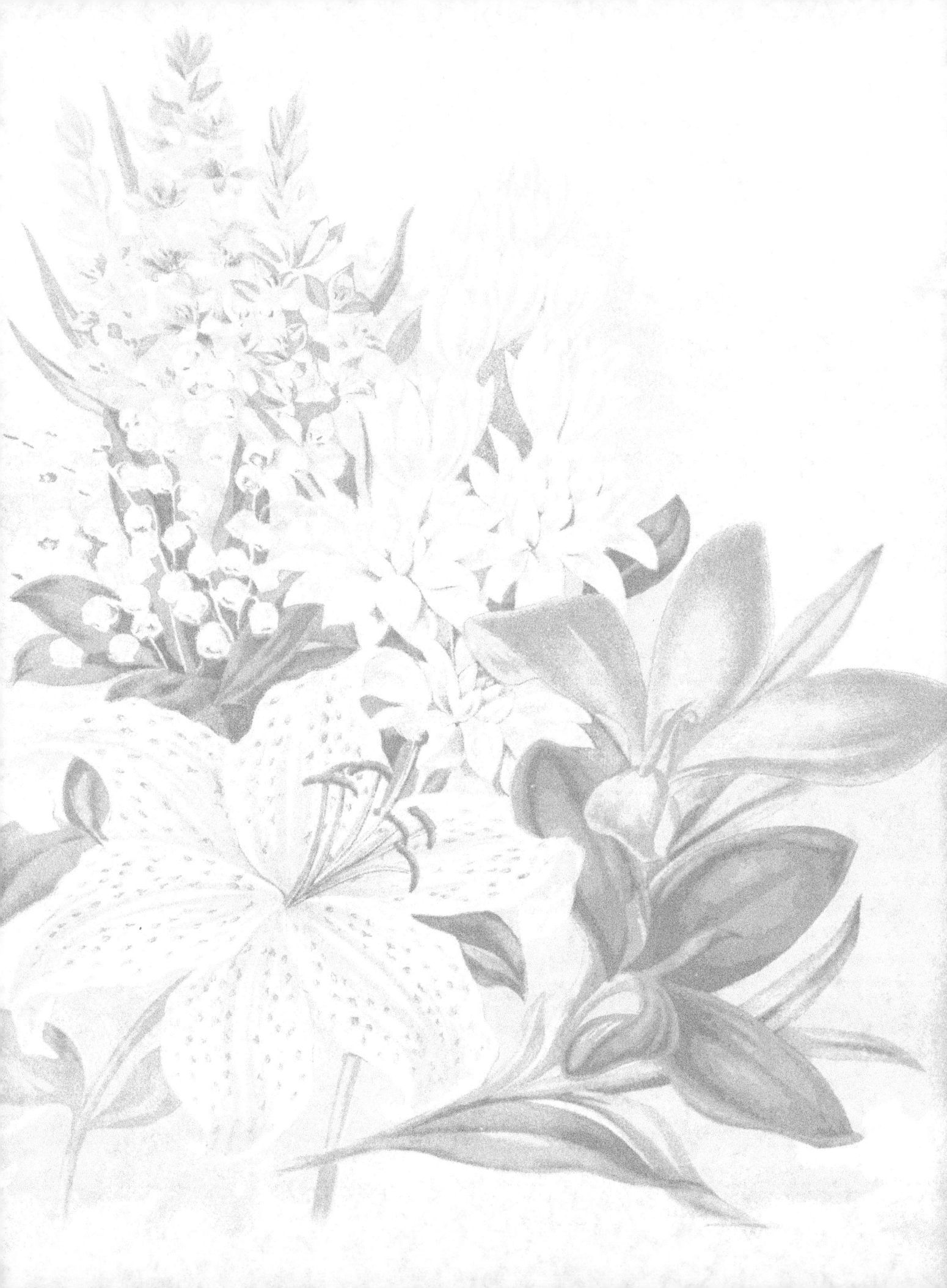

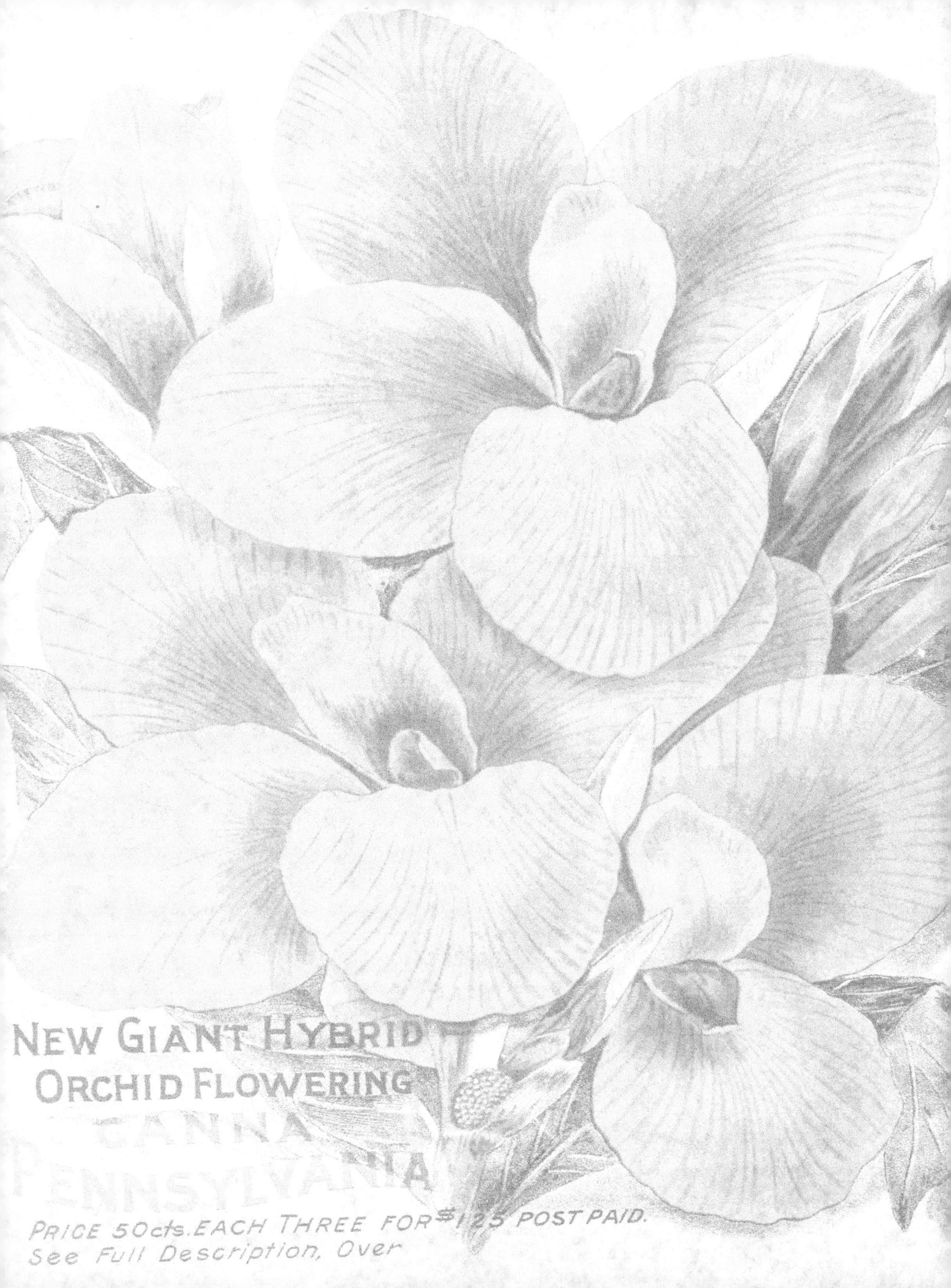

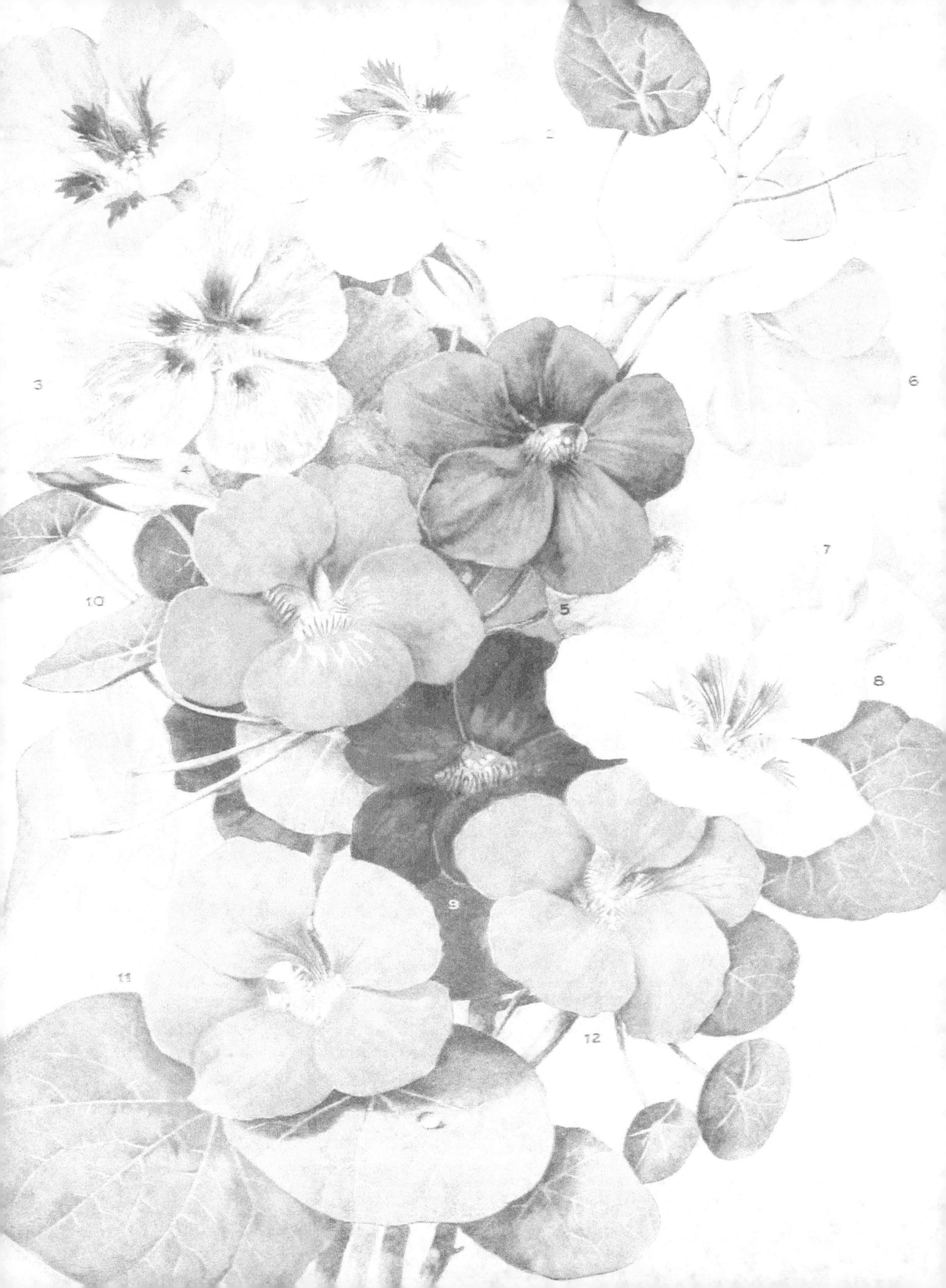

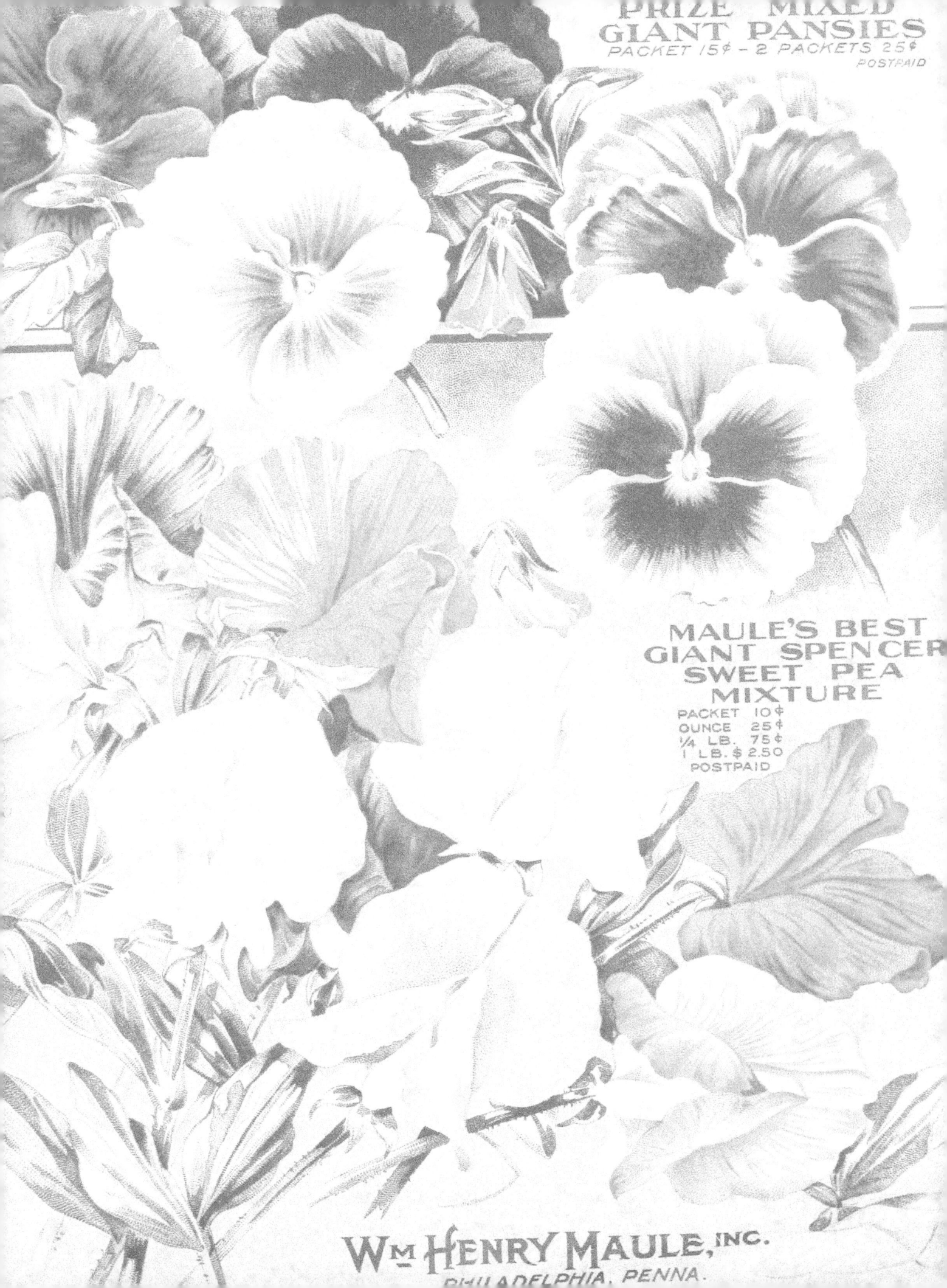

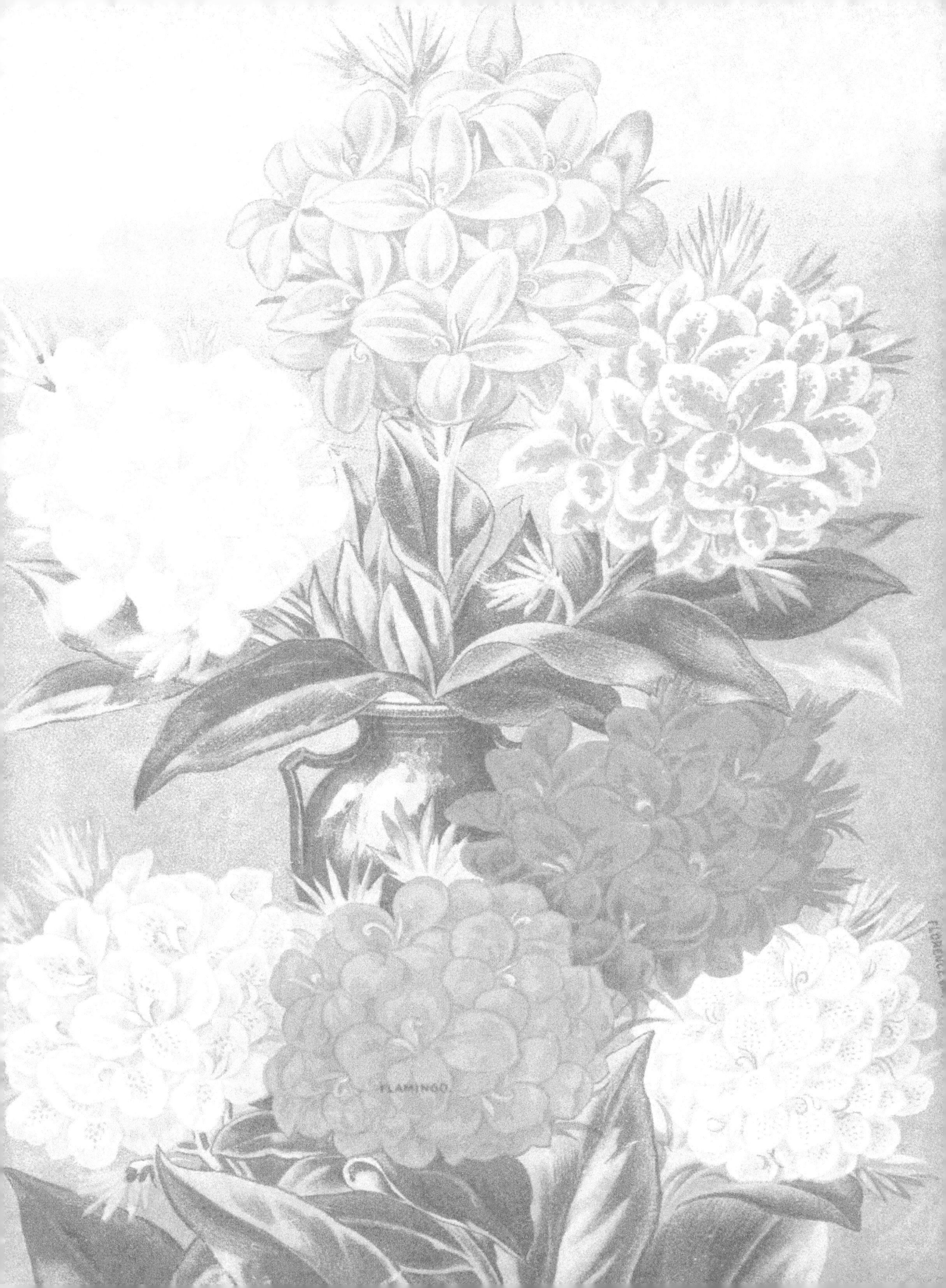

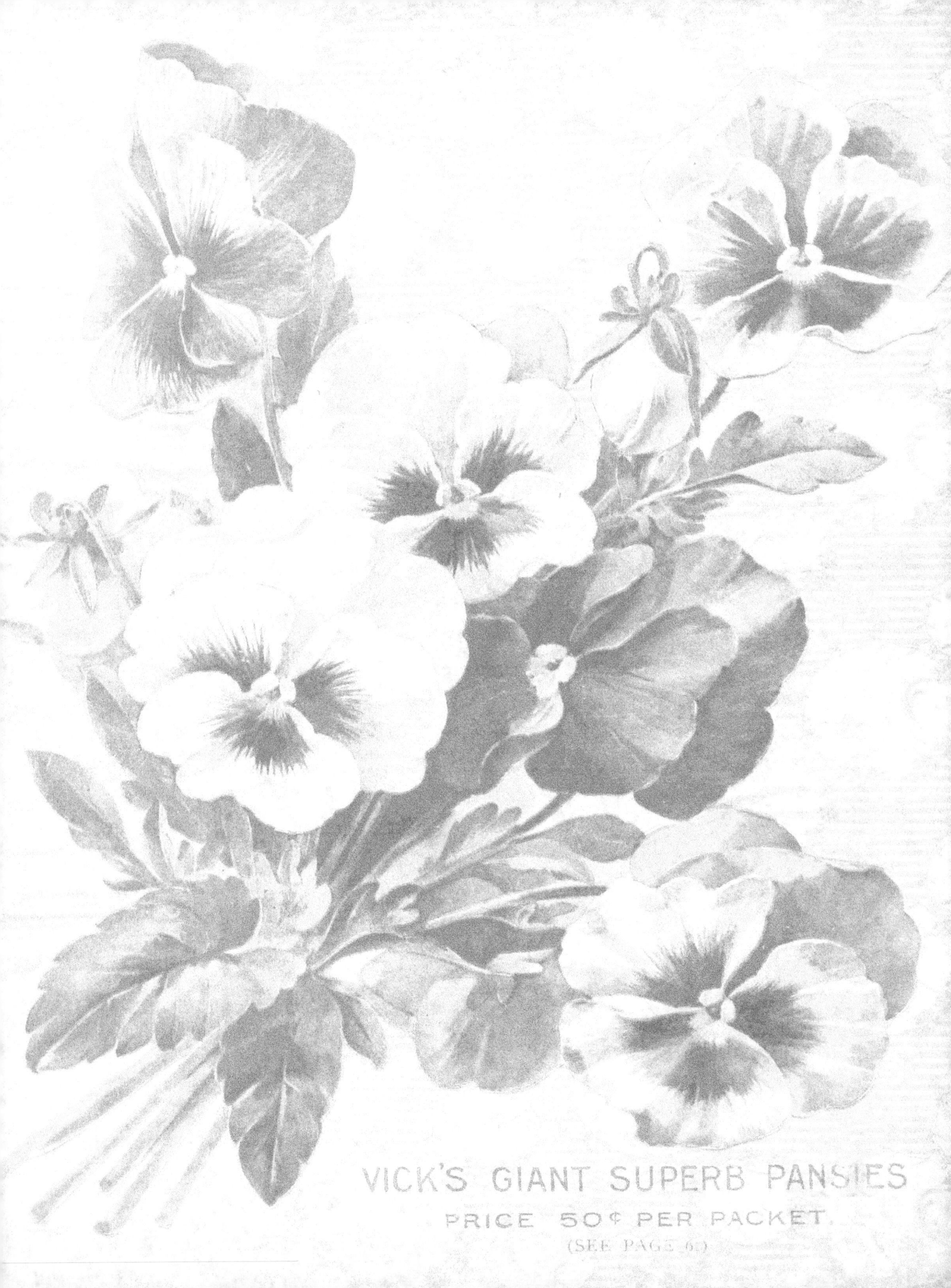

VICK'S GIANT SUPERB PANSIES
PRICE 50¢ PER PACKET
(SEE PAGE 6)

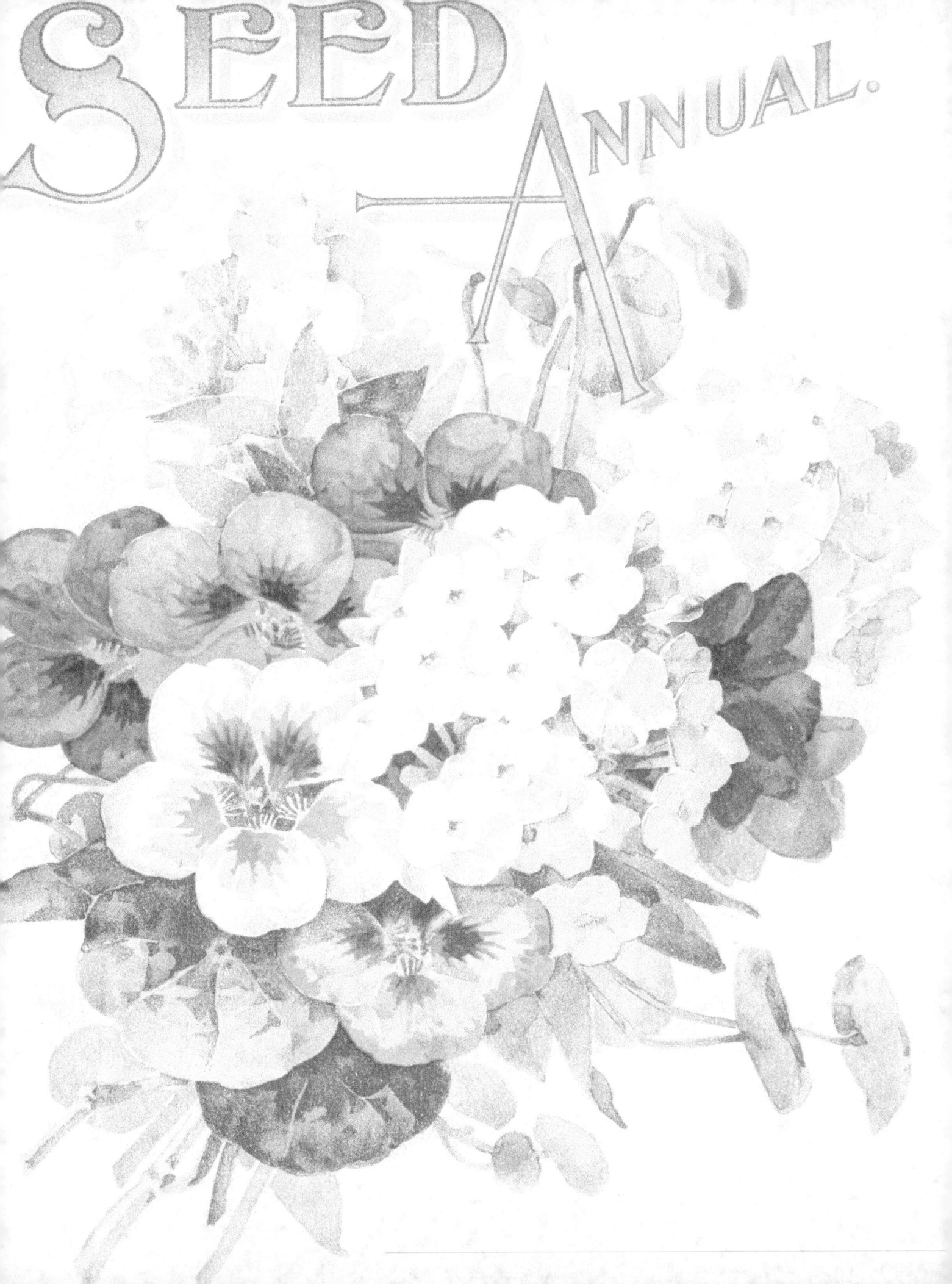

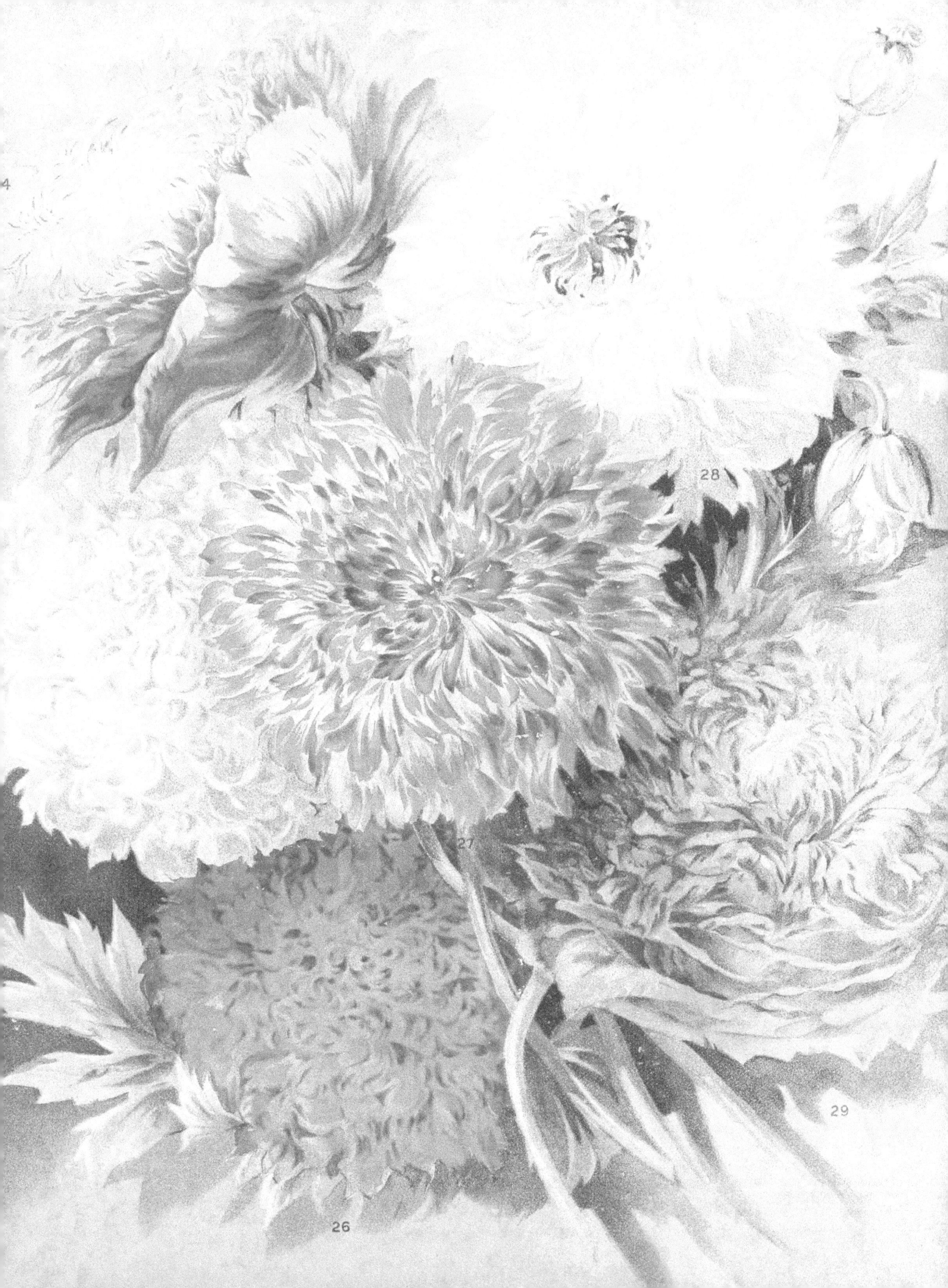

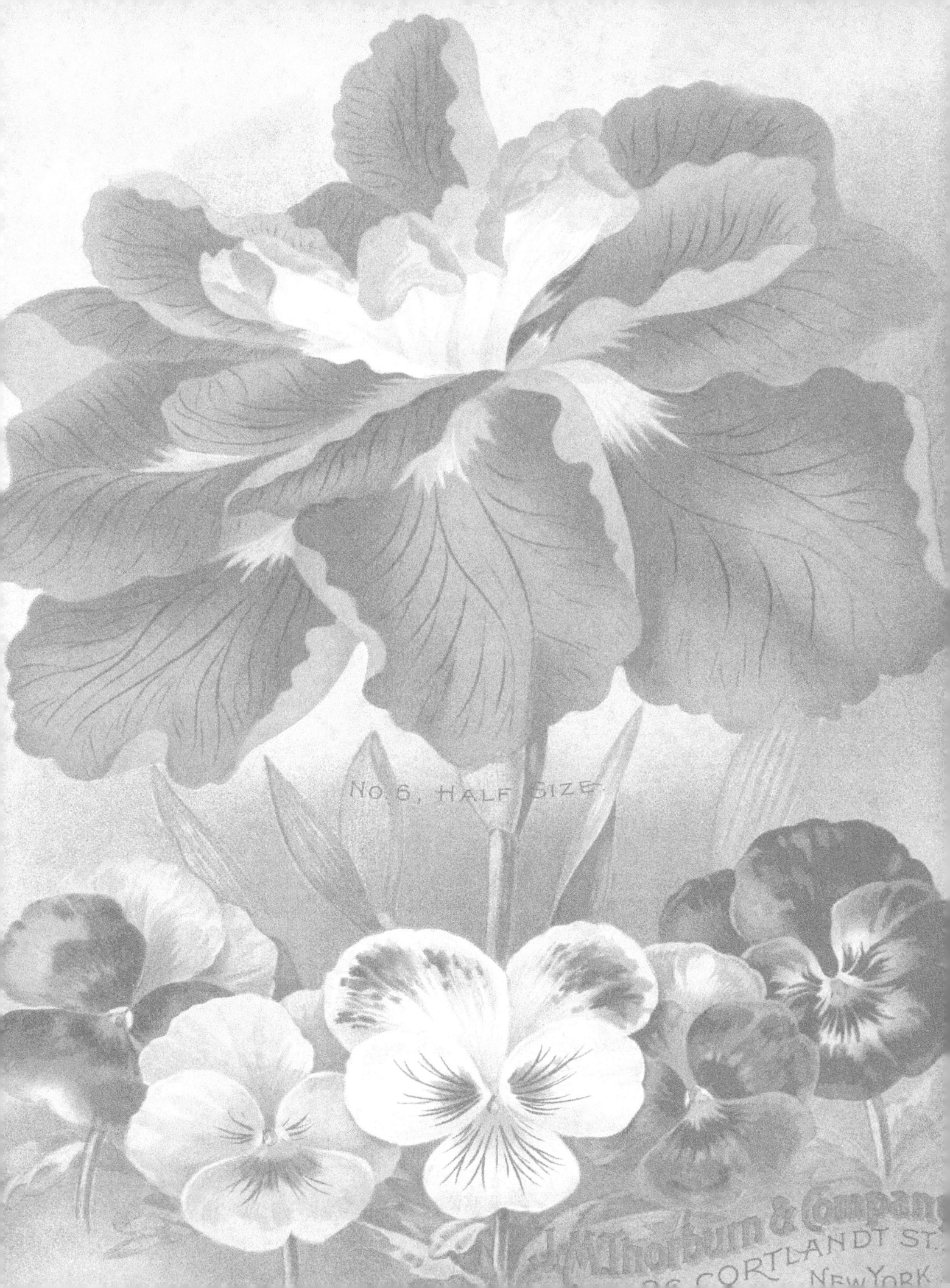

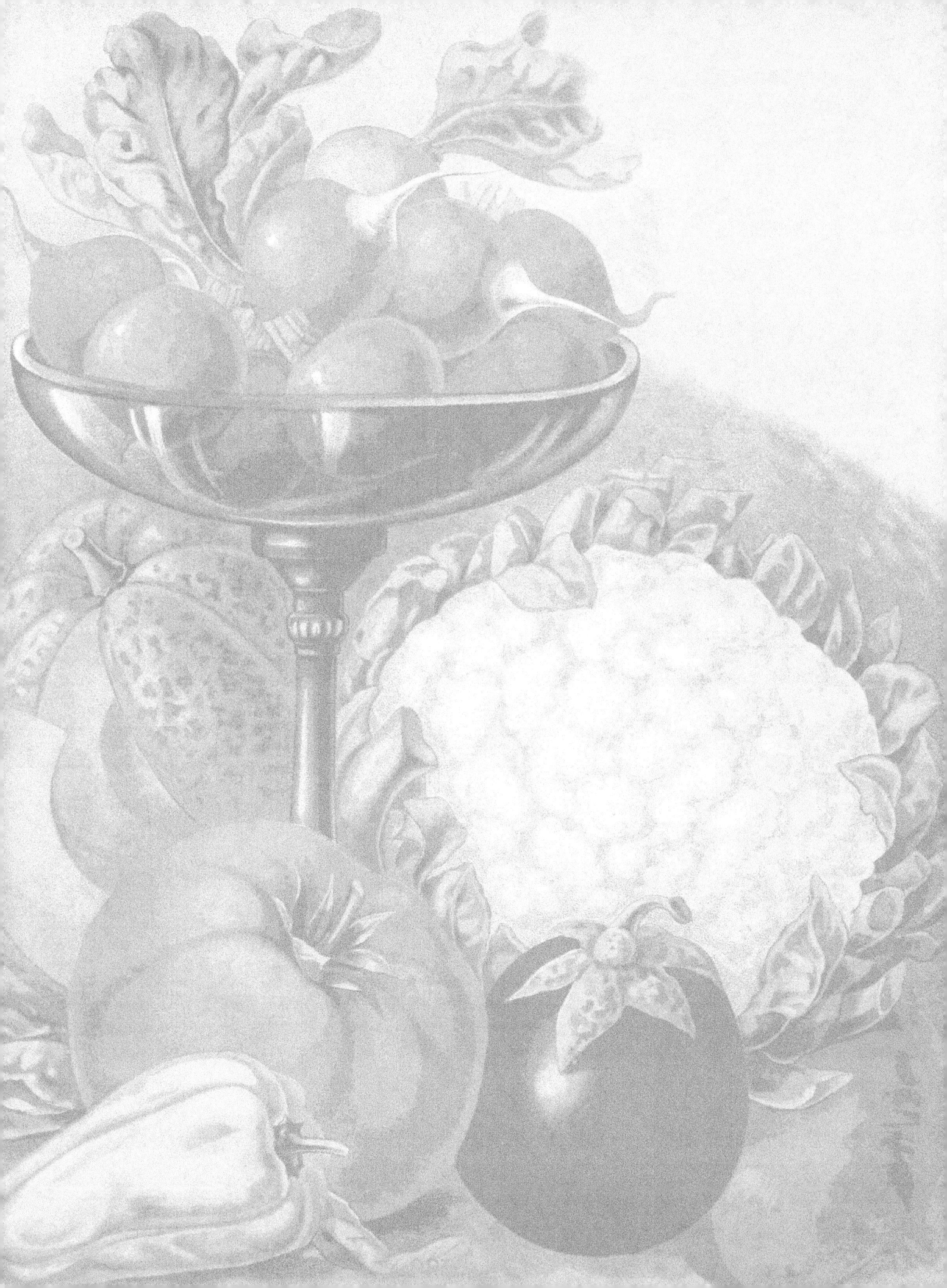

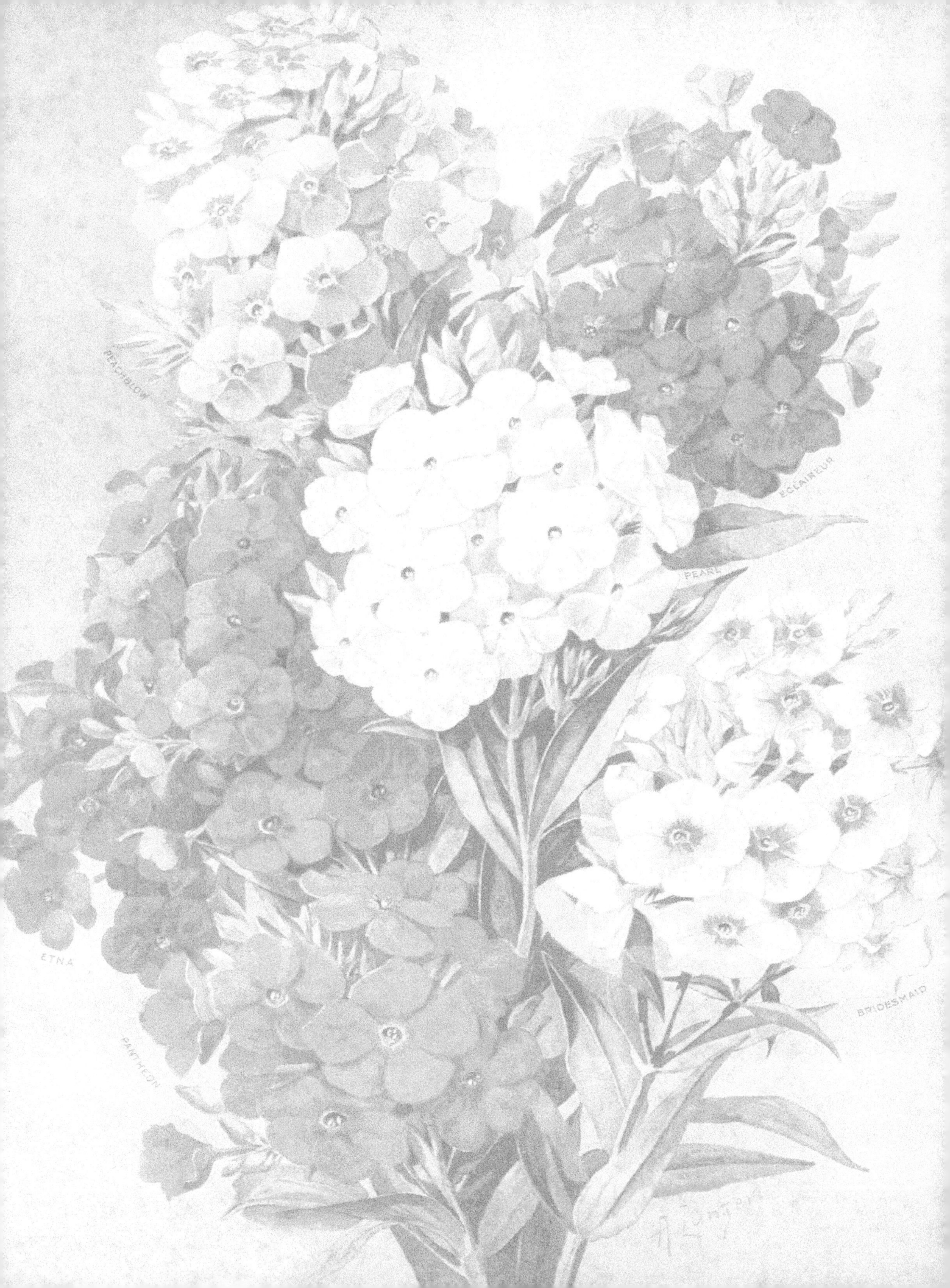

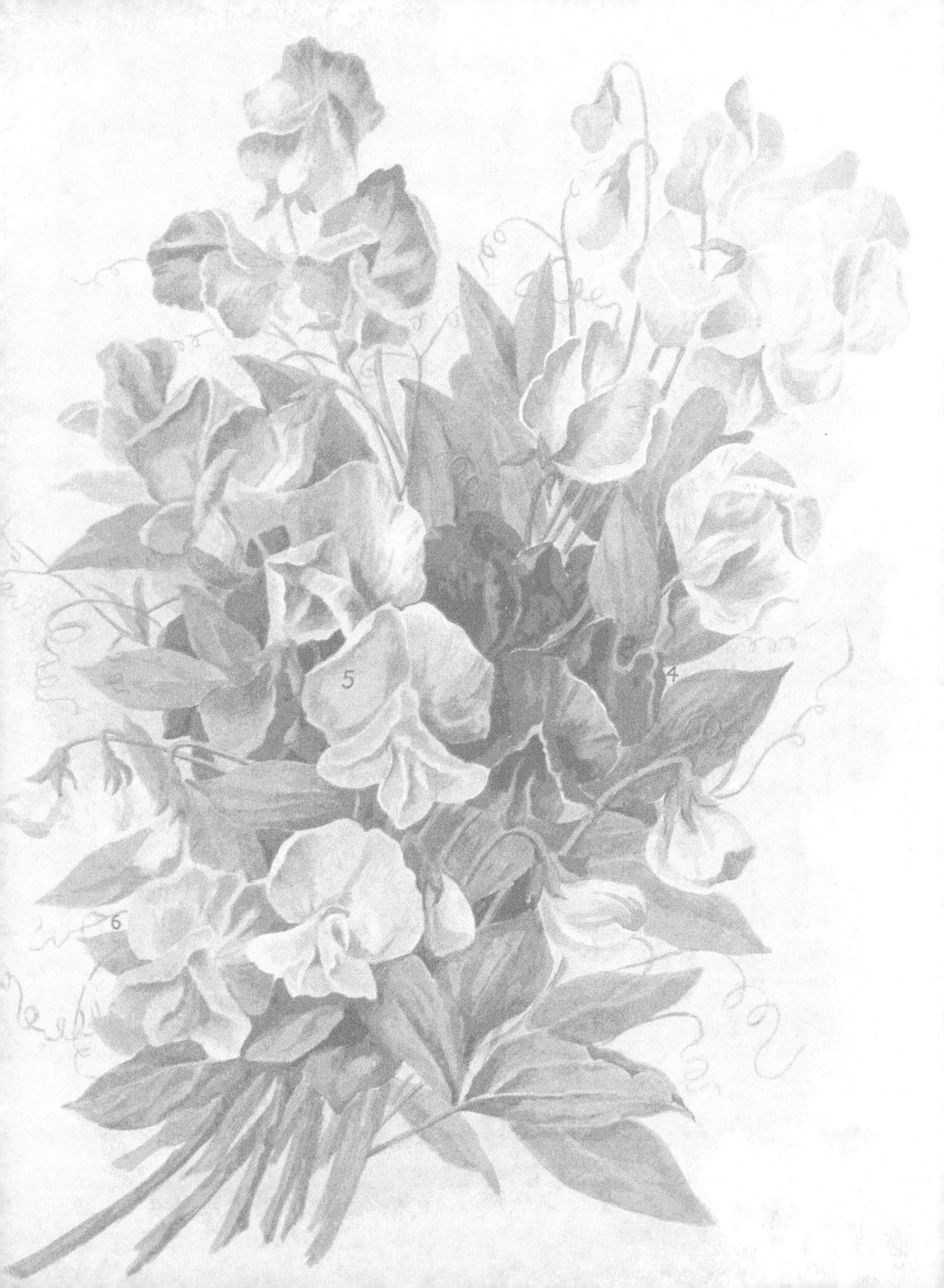

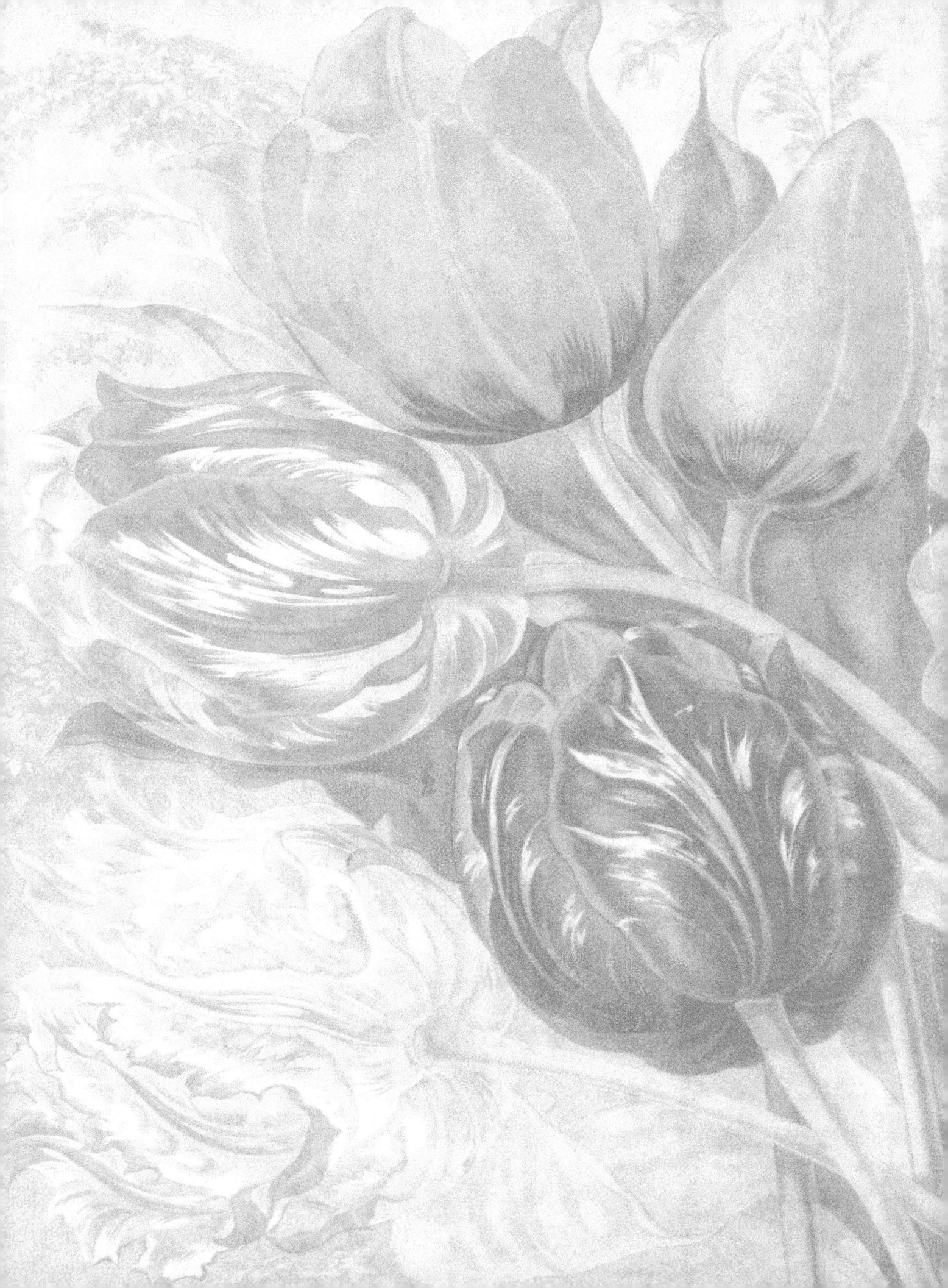

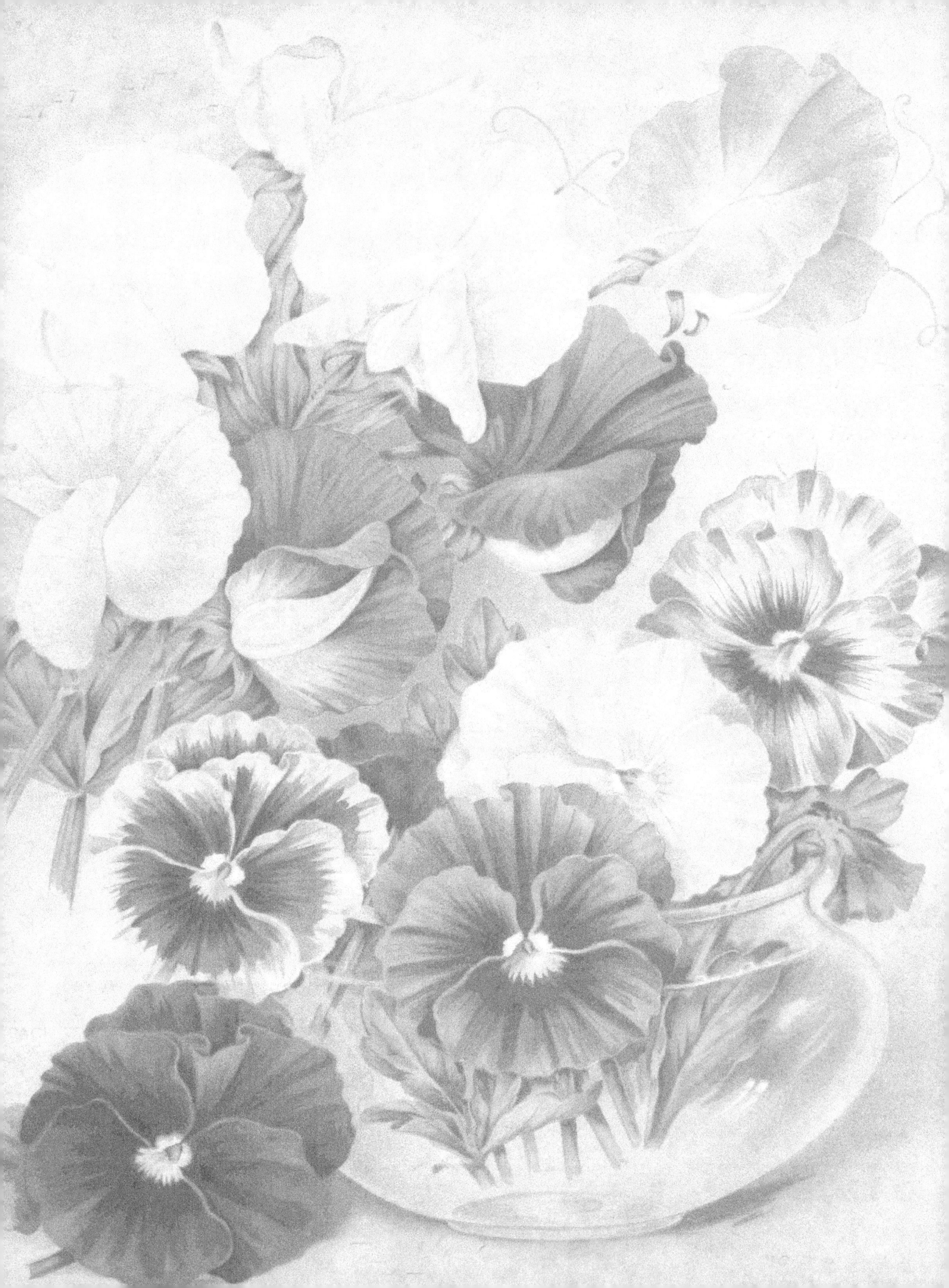

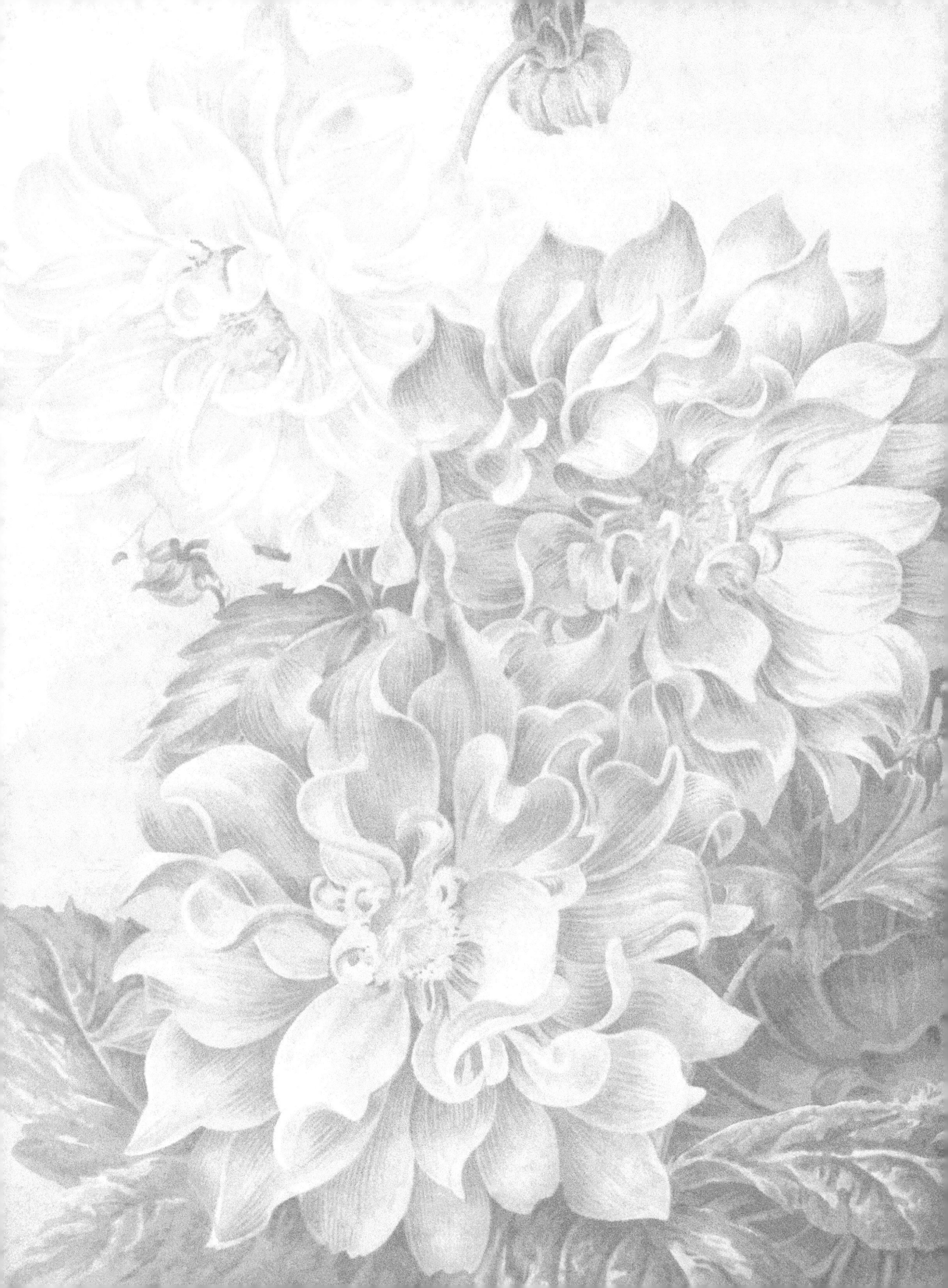

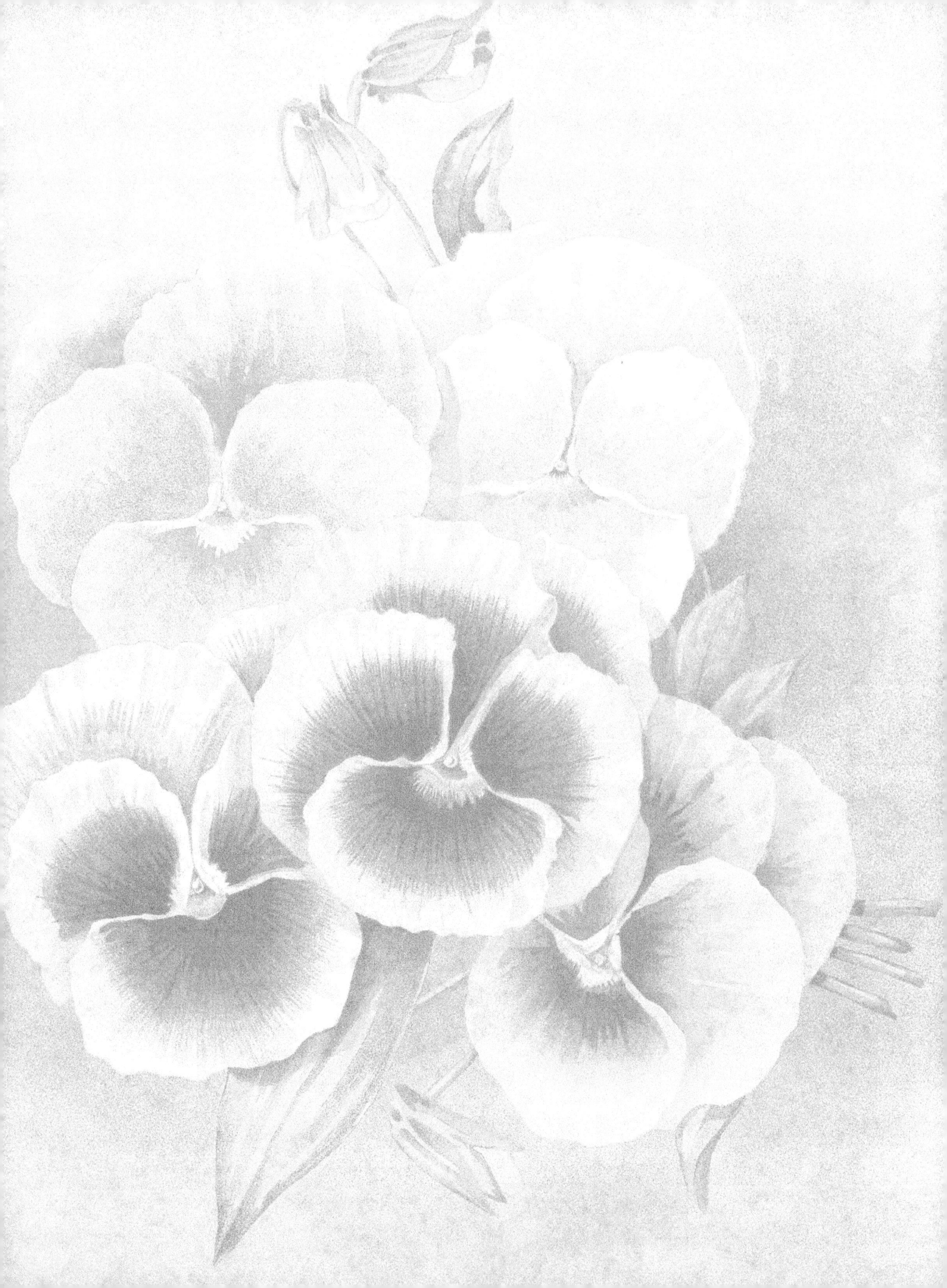

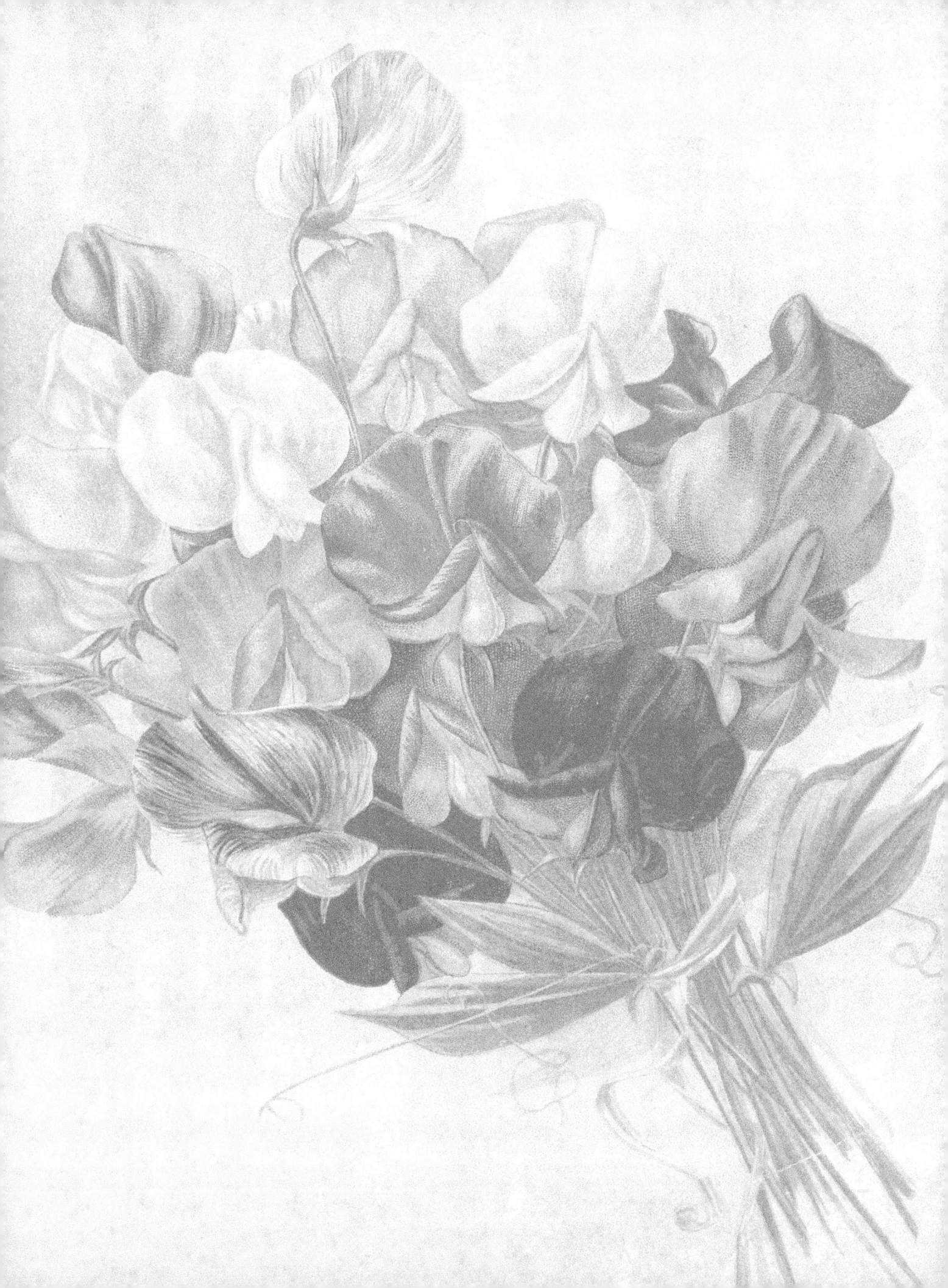

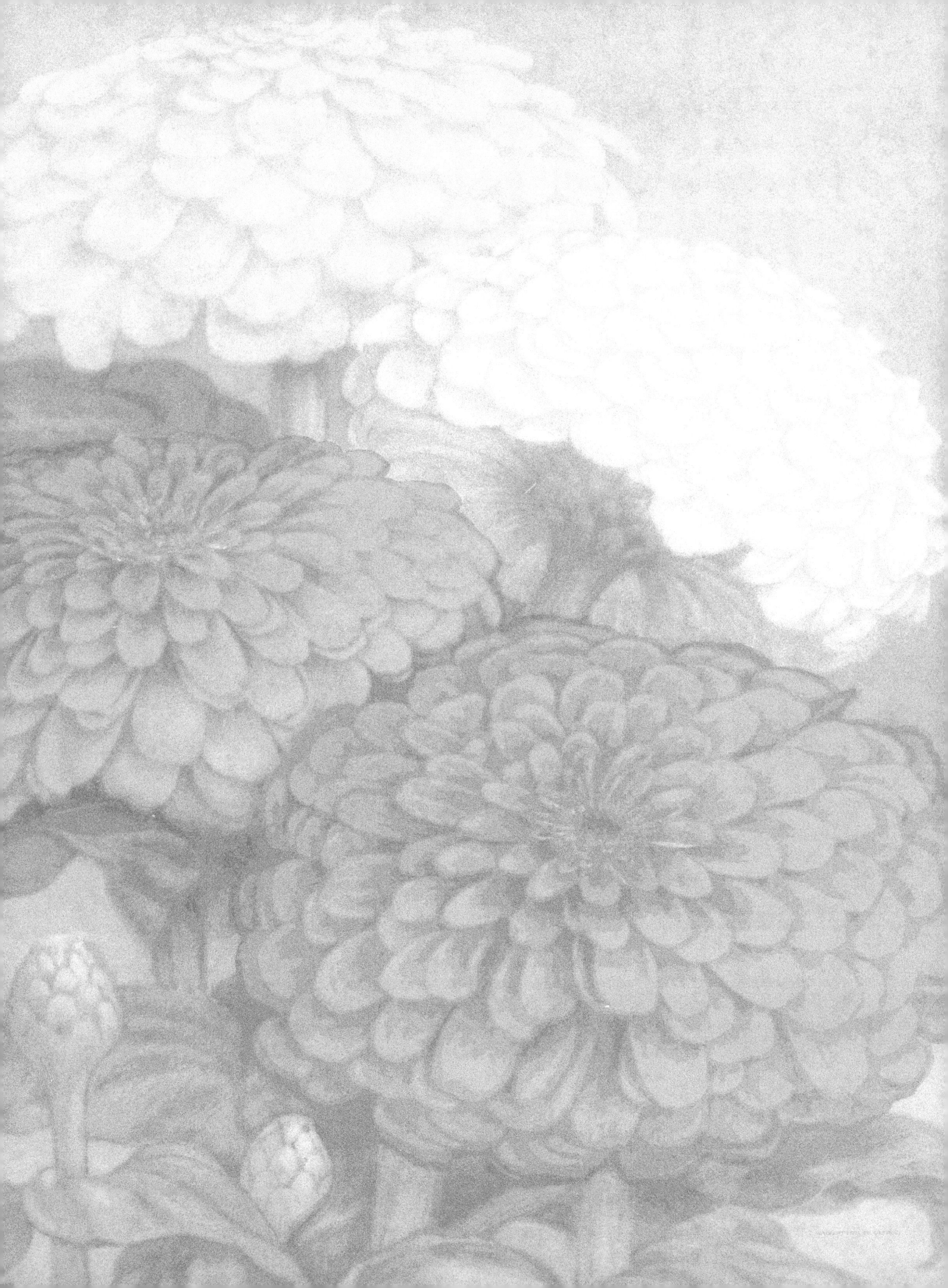

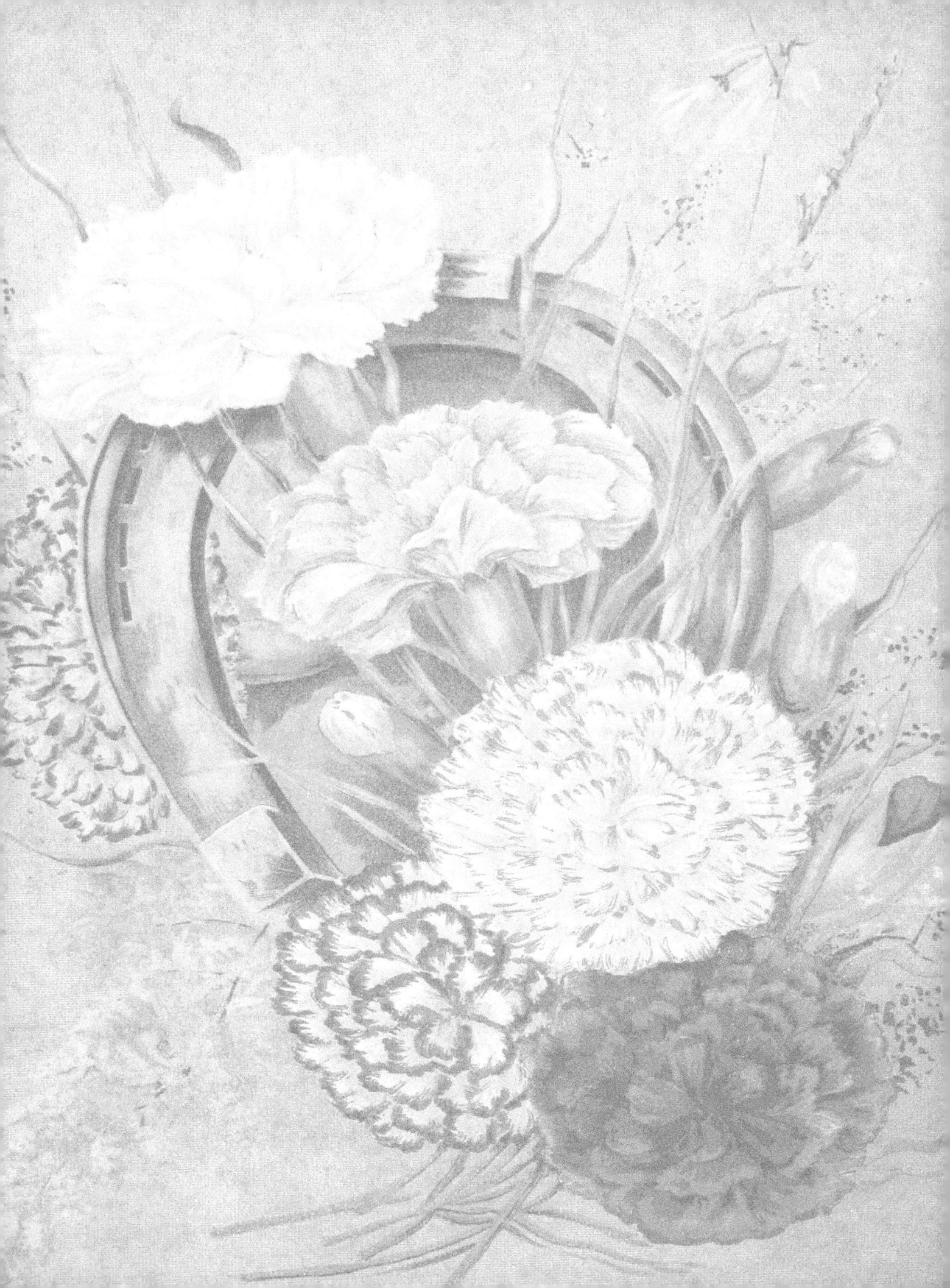

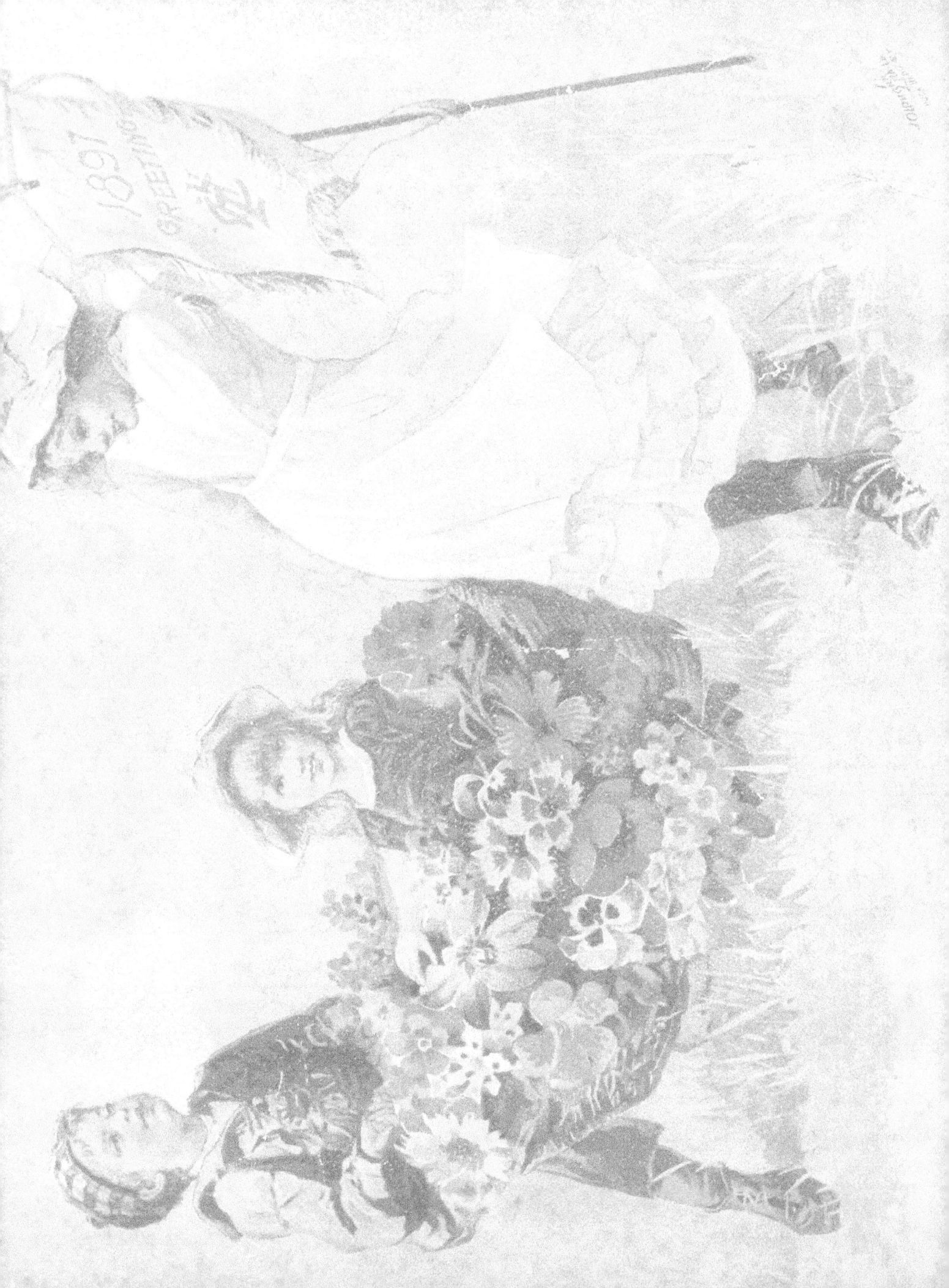

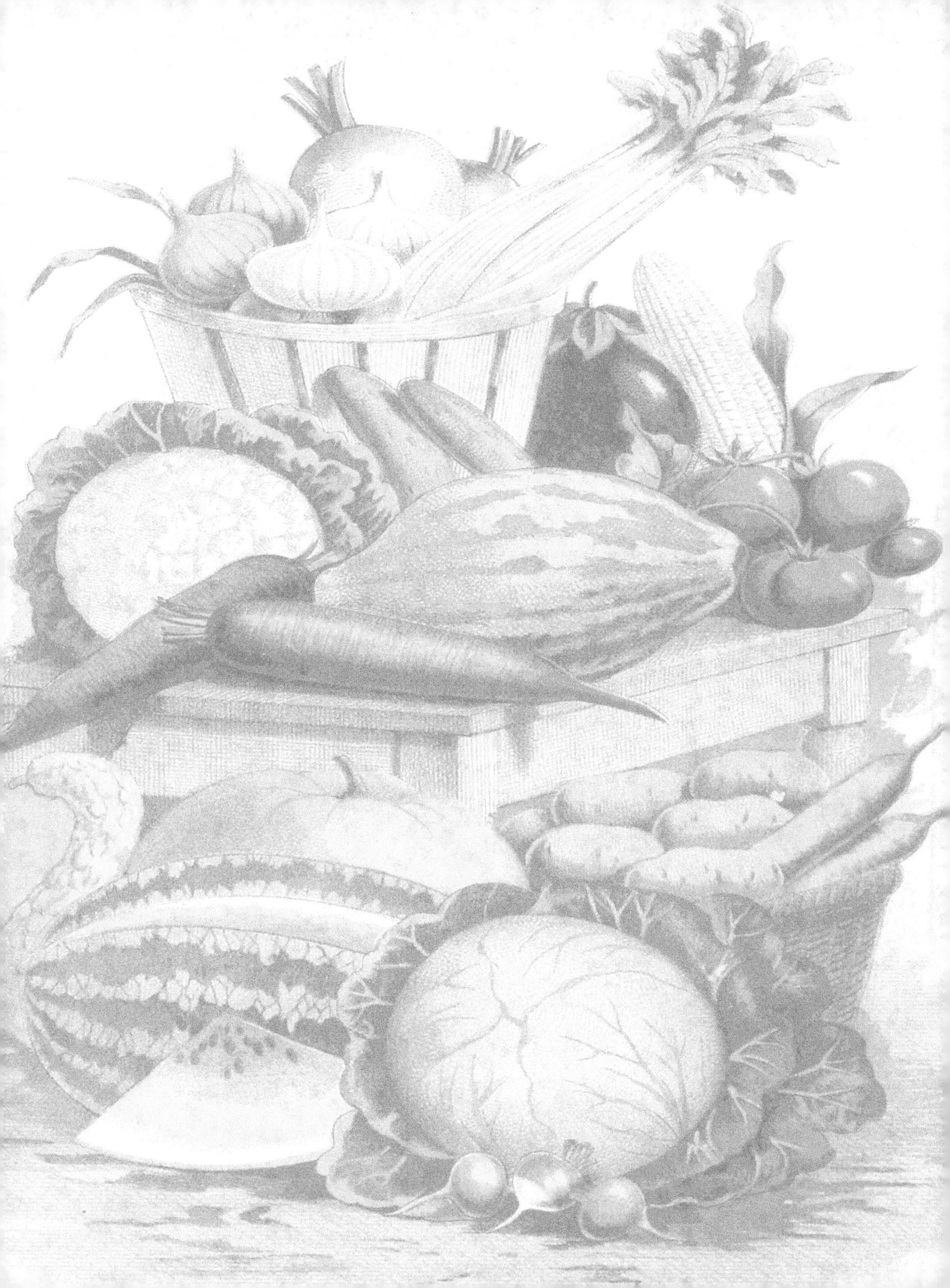

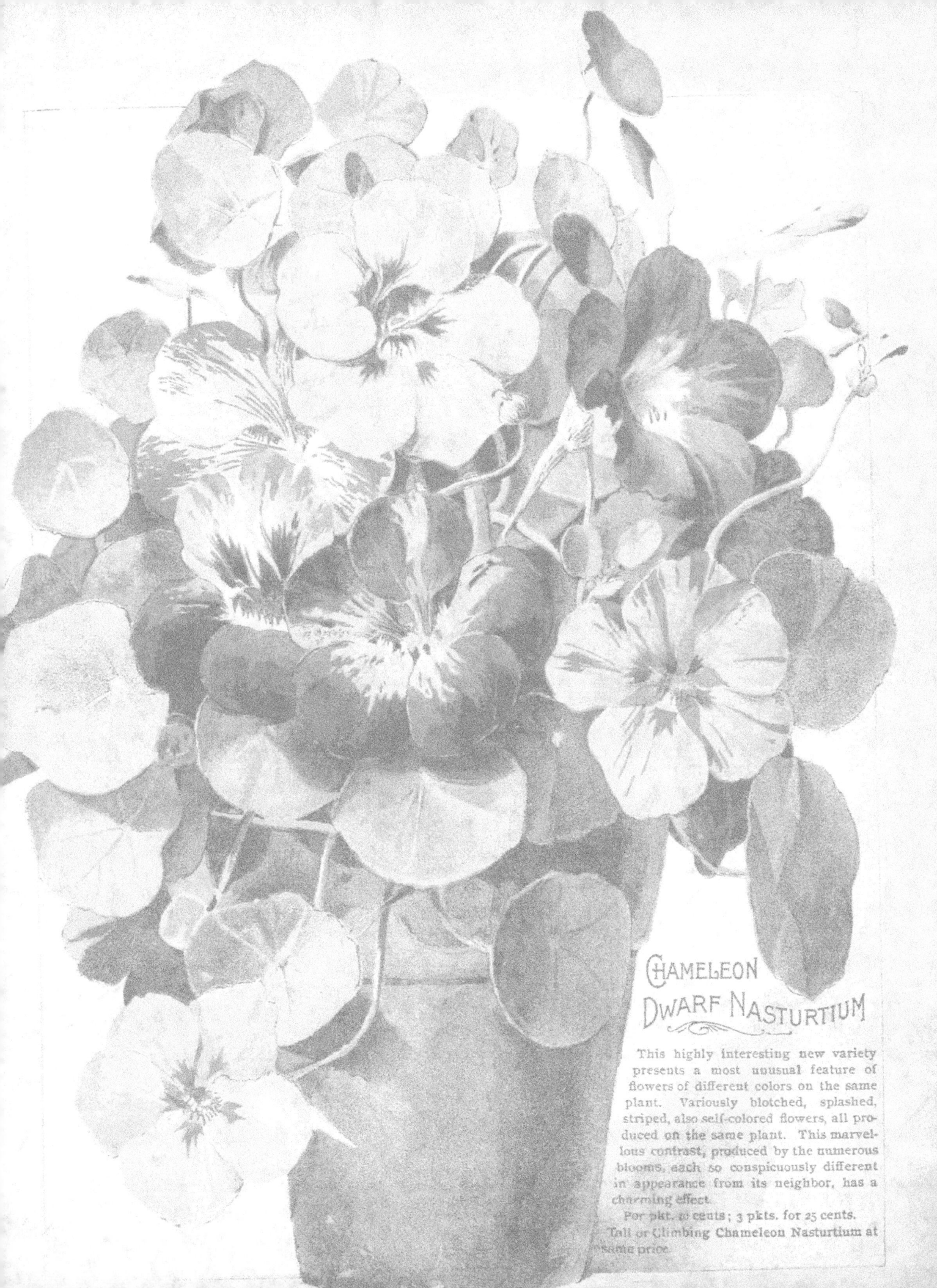

Chameleon Dwarf Nasturtium

This highly interesting new variety presents a most unusual feature of flowers of different colors on the same plant. Variously blotched, splashed, striped, also self-colored flowers, all produced on the same plant. This marvellous contrast, produced by the numerous blooms, each so conspicuously different in appearance from its neighbor, has a charming effect.

Per pkt. 10 cents; 3 pkts. for 25 cents. Tall or Climbing Chameleon Nasturtium at same price.

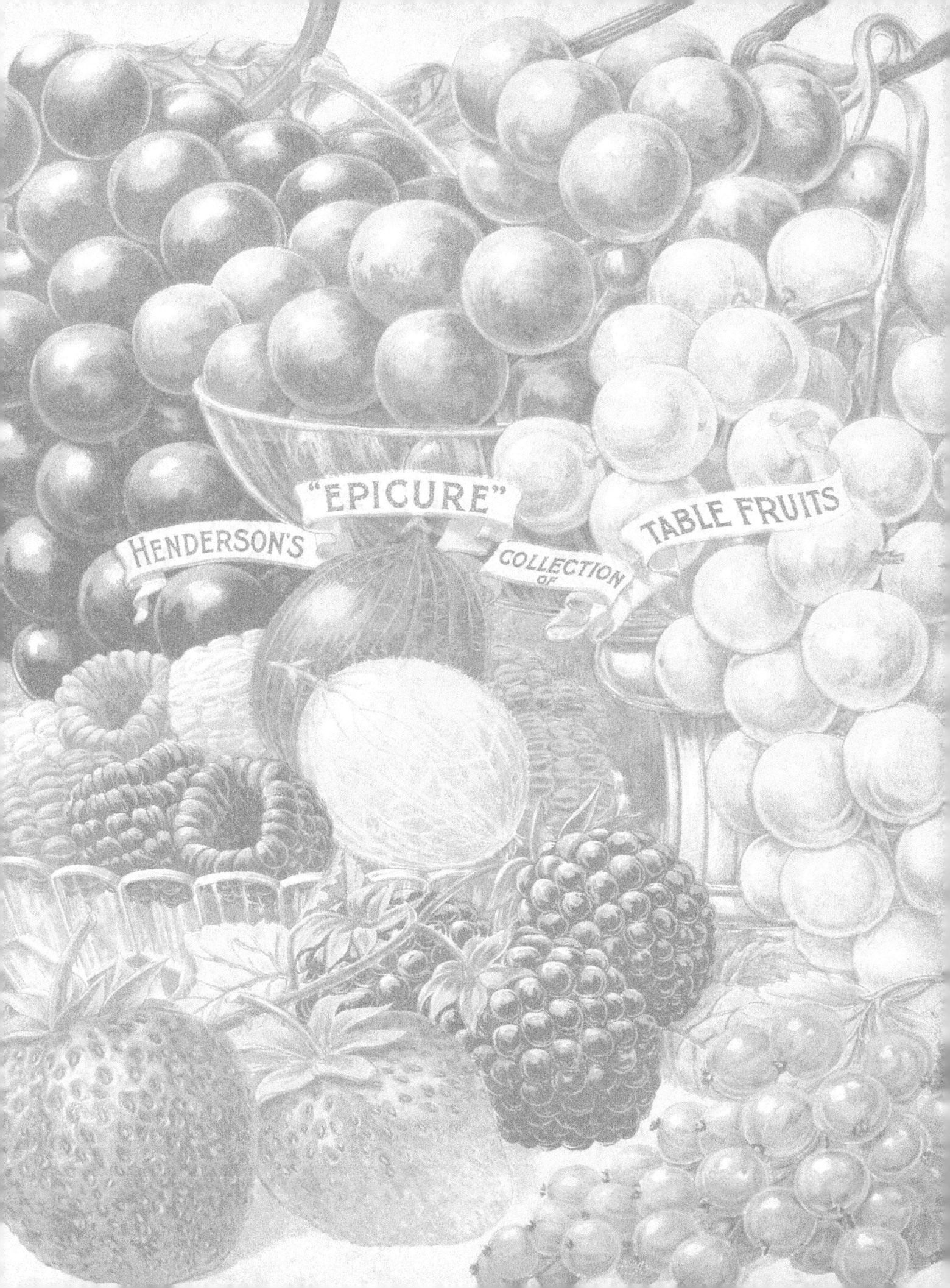

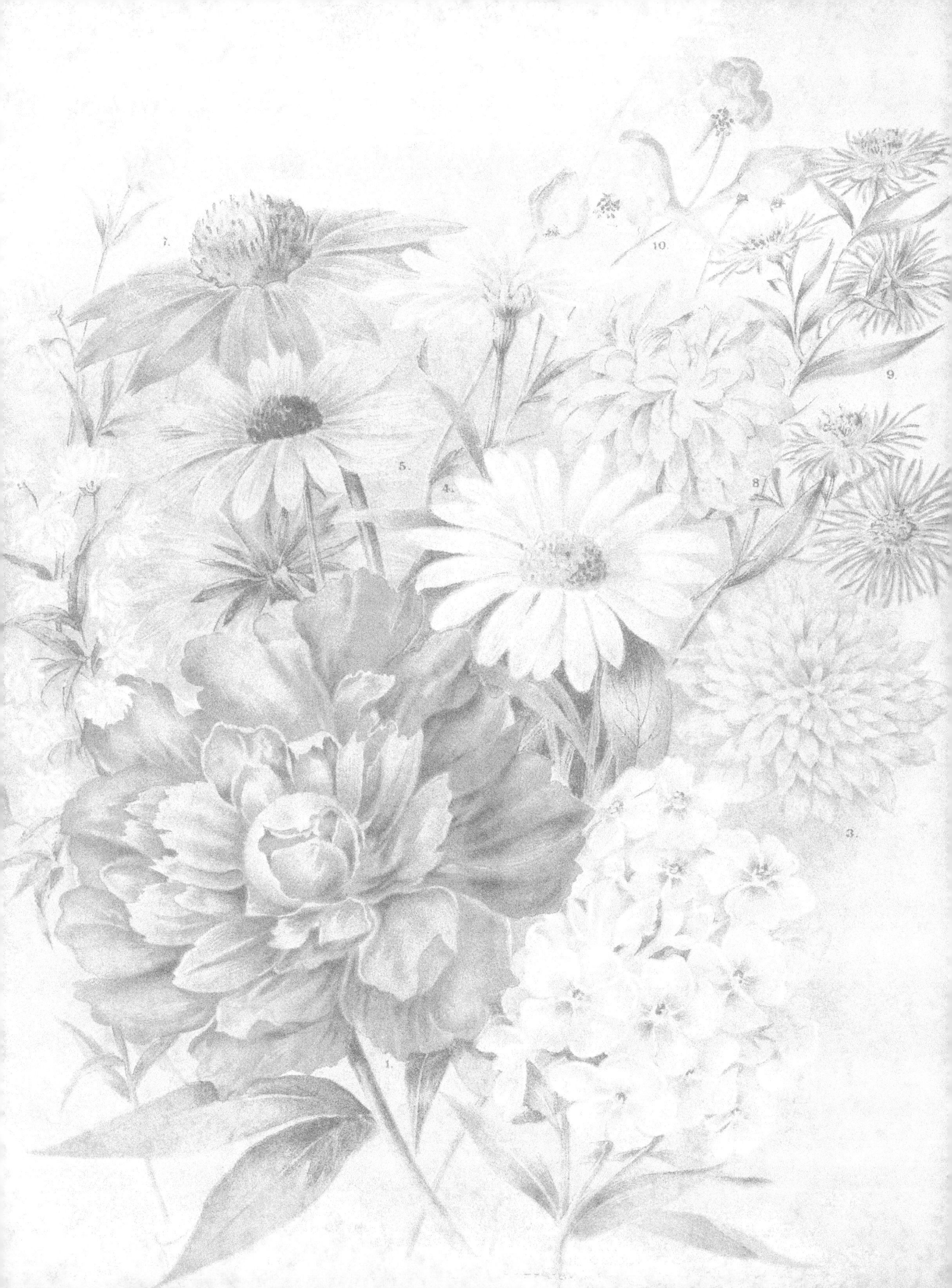

PURPUREA
PKT. 20¢

CARMINEA
PKT. 20¢

SALMONEA
PKT. 20¢

MAULE'S PRIZE GIANT MIXED PANSIES
Packet 15¢
2 Packets 25¢
POSTPAID

Wm Henry Maule,
PHILADELPHIA, PENNA.

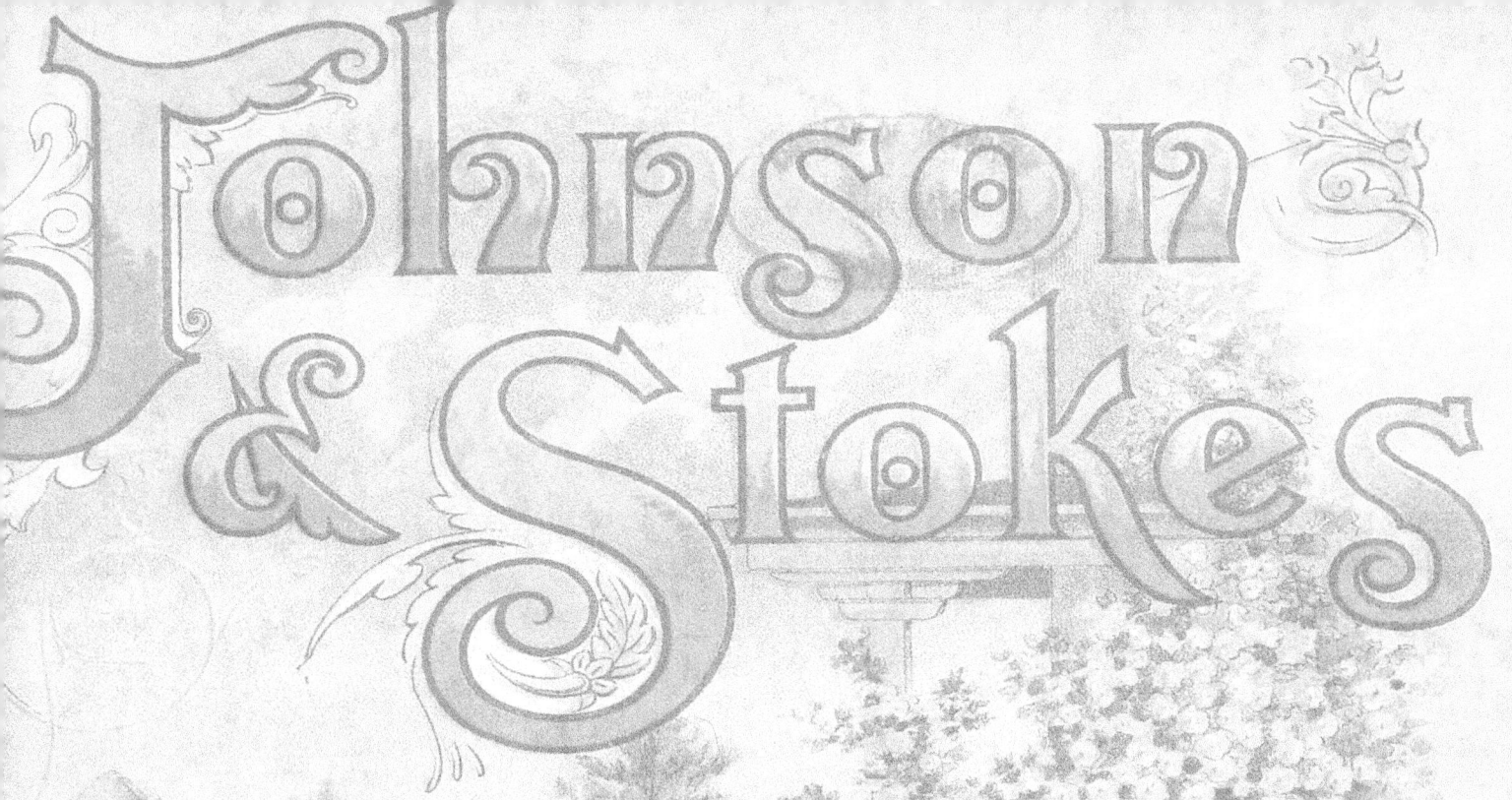

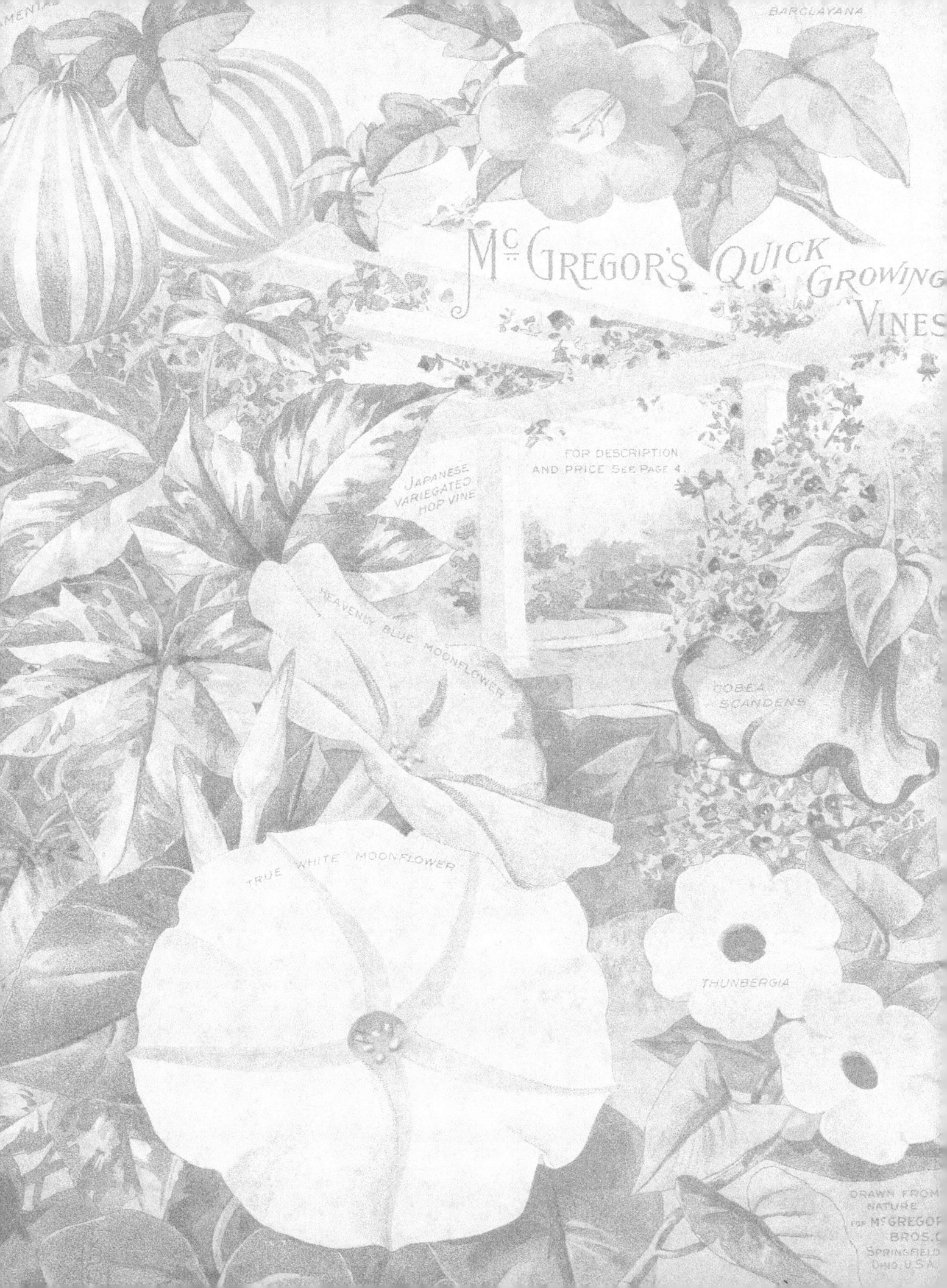

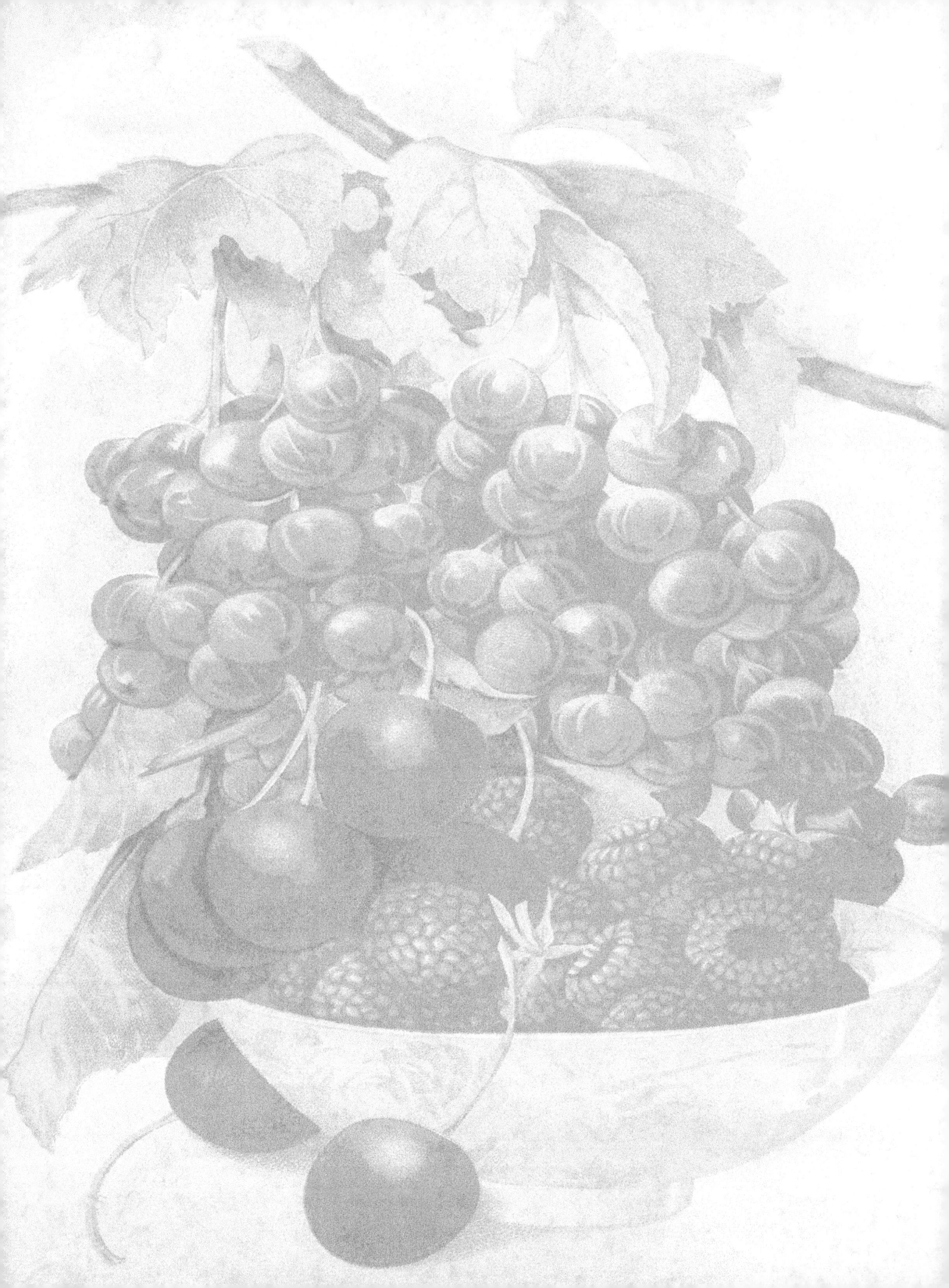

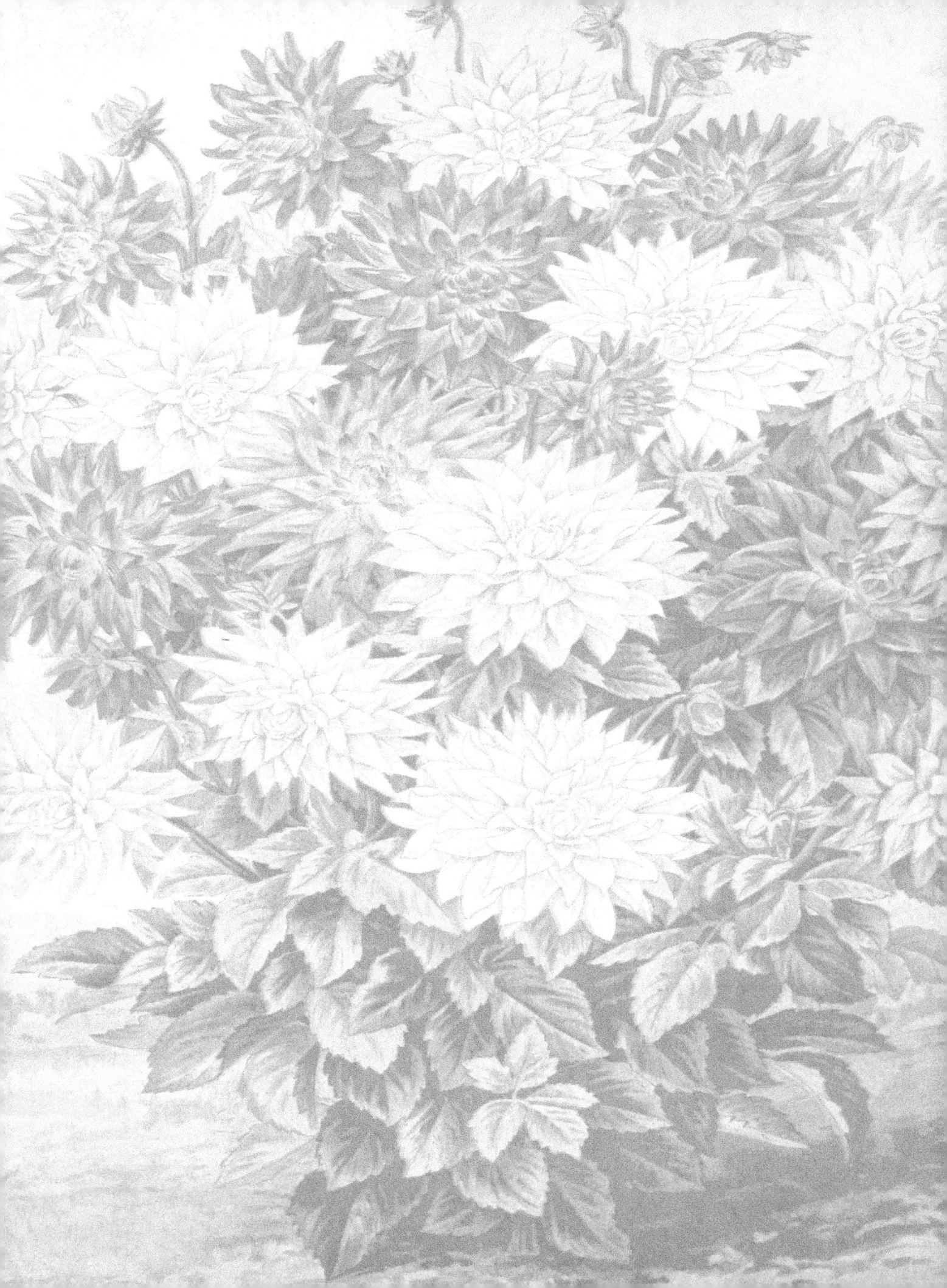

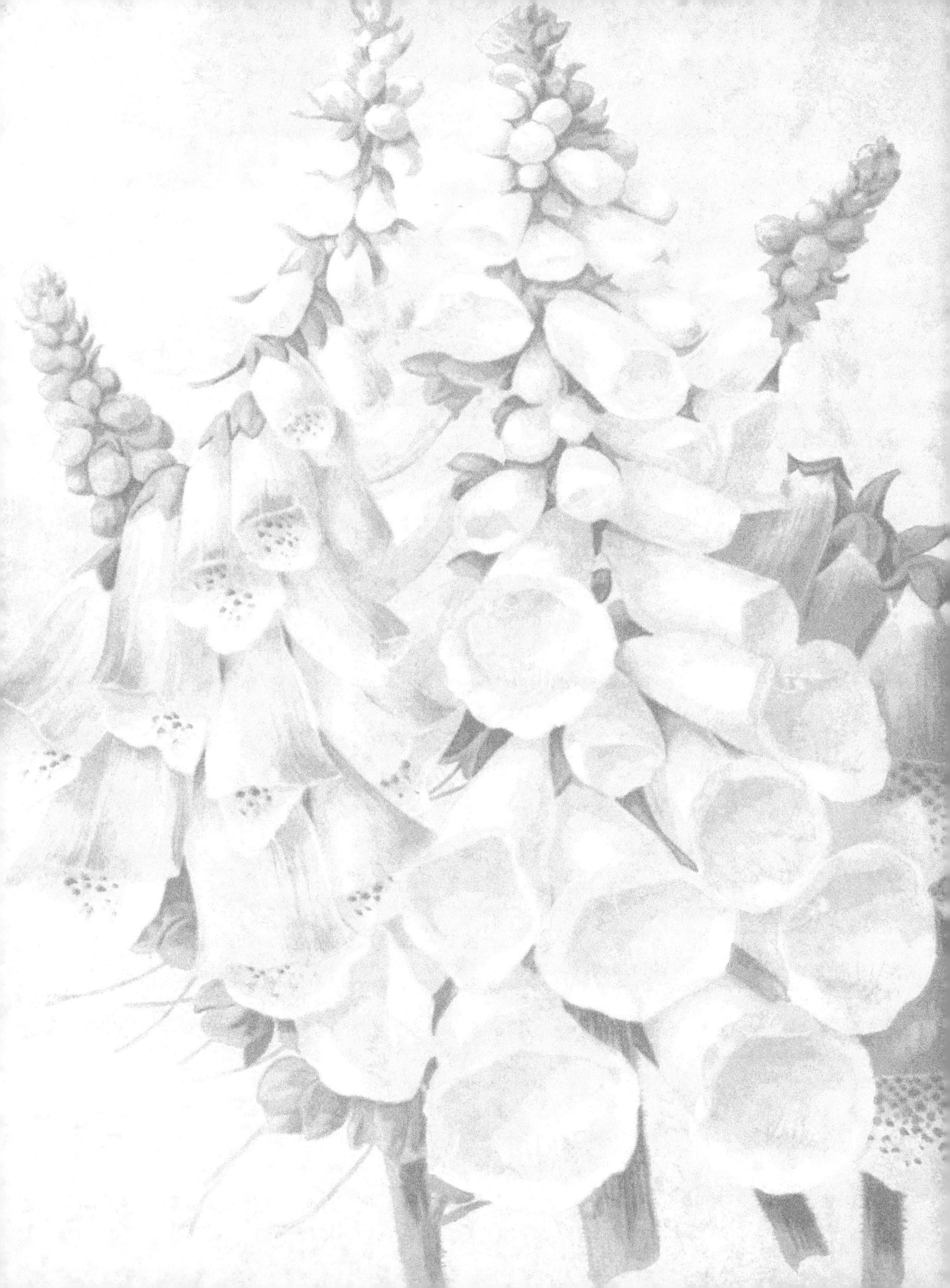

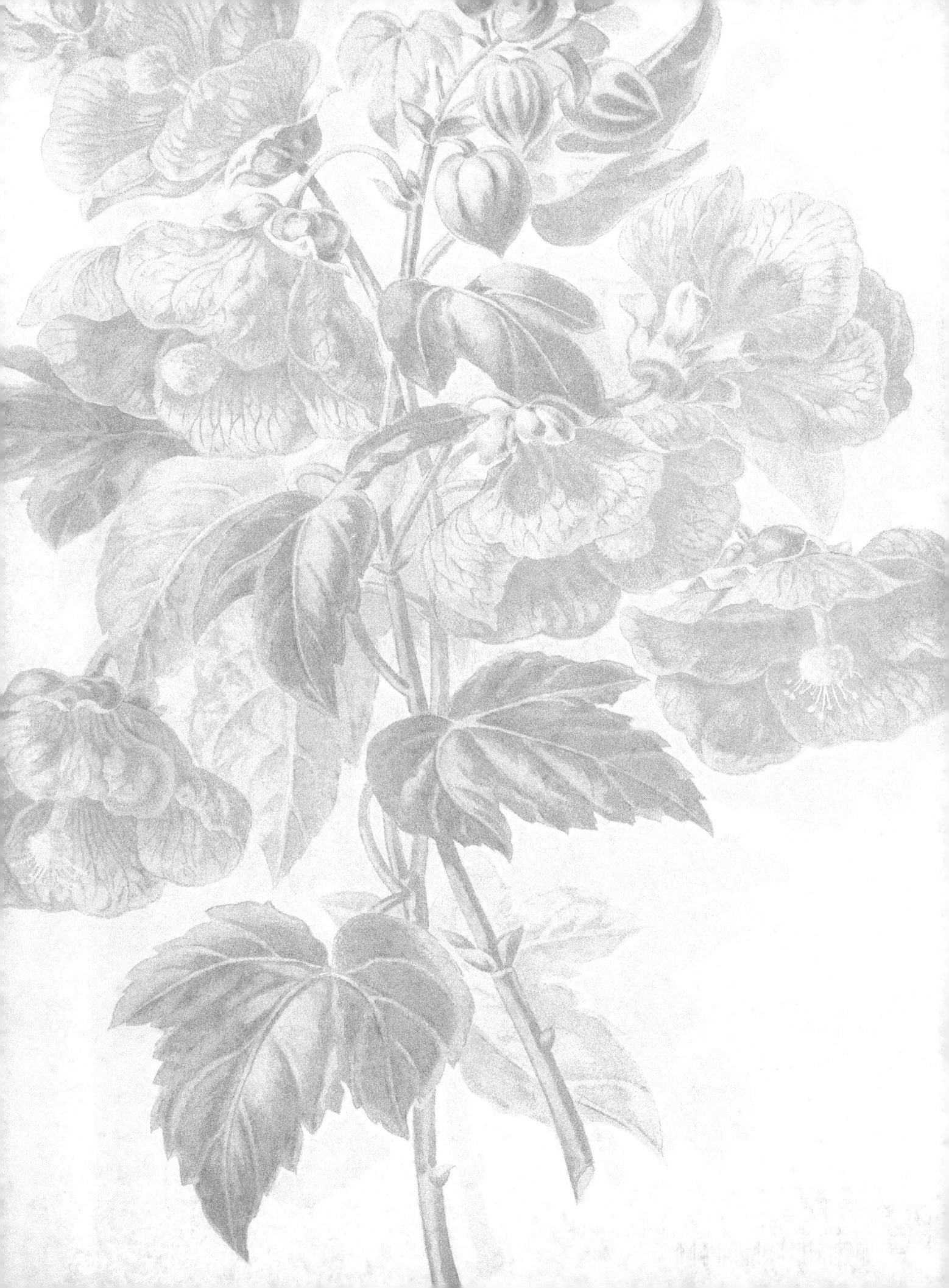

www.ingramcontent.com/pod-product-compliance
Lightning Source LLC
Chambersburg PA
CBHW060426220526
45465CB00008B/3033